Claudia Roden was born in Cairo and spent her early years in the Arab world, where coffee originated and where it is still the most important drink. She finished her education in Paris and England and studied at St Martin's School of Art in London. Starting as a painter, she was drawn to the subject of food partly through a desire to recreate a lost heritage — one of the pleasures of a happy life in Egypt. The local delight in food, like the light, colour and smells and the special brand of hospitality, warmth and humour, has left a permanent impression.

Her first venture into cookery, *A Book of Middle Eastern Food*, was published in 1968. She has continued to write about food, with a special interest in the social and historical background of cooking, contributing to various publications, including *Le Monde*, *Gourmet Magazine* and the *Sunday Times*, as well as to several books. She has also lectured, demonstrated and taught cooking. Her latest publication is a book on outdoor cookery, *Picnic* (1981).

Claudia Roden lives in London with her three grown-up children.

COFFEE

Claudia Roden

PENGUIN BOOKS

Penguin Books Ltd, Harmondsworth, Middlesex, England
Penguin Books, 625 Madison Avenue, New York, New York 10022, U.S.A.
Penguin Books Australia Ltd, Ringwood, Victoria, Australia
Penguin Books Canada Ltd, 2801 John Street, Markham, Ontario, Canada L3R 1B4
Penguin Books (N.Z.) Ltd, 182-190 Wairau Road, Auckland 10, New Zealand

—

First published by Faber and Faber 1977
Published in Penguin Books 1981

—

—

Made and printed in Great Britain by
Cox & Wyman Ltd, Reading

To my father and mother

Contents

Acknowledgements

I wish to thank the many friends who have talked to me about coffee. I gratefully acknowledge the help of my brother Zaki with his ready and generous advice, of Nancy Hibbs who kindly typed my manuscript, of Suzette Macedo for access to Ukers' *All About Coffee*, of my editors, Rosemary Goad and Eileen Brooksbank, for their sympathetic appreciation and gentle encouragement. I am especially thankful to Tony Santos for his early enthusiasm for the project and for generously allowing us to use the prints from his collection. For information about coffee, I wish to thank Kerry Muir of the International Coffee Organisation, Mr. A. W. Ayling of Lyons' Sol Café Ltd., Mr. Silvio Lima of the Brazilian Coffee Institute, Mr. Arl of Appleton, Machin and Smiles; and the late George Markus of the Markus Coffee Co. Ltd. in Connaught Street, and his daughter Mari who were so generous. Most of all I am indebted to my friend Barbara Maher for her enthusiastic encouragement and advice, and for tasting and reading and re-reading. Her help throughout has been invaluable. My thanks also to my children Simon, Nadia and Anna for being lovely while I worked—they have asked me to thank them!

The line illustrations between pages 84 and 94 are drawn by Nadia Roden.

Introduction

I have loved coffee ever since, as young children in Cairo, we waited outside my parents' bedroom door for signs of their awakening. When the shadows on the frosted glass began to move, a signal and an invitation to come in, we pounced and raced for the coveted places in the large double bed where we waited for the coffee ritual to start.

Maria, our Yugoslav nanny and housekeeper, brought in a large brass tray ornately engraved in praise of Allah, on which were placed five small cups in delicate bone china with gold arabesques near the rim. A glass of water held a piece of ice chipped from the block in the ice box, and was scented with a drop of orange flower water. A small plate carried a pile of oriental petits fours filled with dates, pistachios or ground almonds. My father poured out the coffee from two small copper *kanakas* (or *ibriks* as they are called in Turkish) with much ceremony, carefully shaking his hand so as to drop a little of the much prized froth in each cup. We passed the water round, then drank the syrupy black brew in little sips and with much reverence.

In Egypt, no one thought children should not drink coffee. It was usually assumed that we would like it sweet, and it was made accordingly and served with home-made preserves and jams. When we had finished, we turned over the tiny cups, for at least one member of the company was reputed to be good at fortune telling. Everything could be read in the grounds: travels, unexpected bequests, weddings. Sometimes the image of a bridegroom-to-be would be seen faintly in the gentle trickle of muddy powder.

My first and favourite coffee was Turkish coffee. Later, travels through Europe and schooldays in France introduced me to *caffè espresso* and *café filtre*.

That coffee has been the marketing success story of recent years in Great Britain may not come as a surprise. But it is curious to note the revolution in drinking habits is merely a return to old styles. Indeed, England was for a time in the seventeenth and eighteenth centuries the greatest coffee drinking country in Europe. Having since lost ground to tea, coffee received comparatively little attention until the Second World War when it saw, apparently as a result of American influence, a gradual return to favour. This new popularity was given a boost by the Italian espresso bar fashion of the Fifties.

However, the recent phenomenal rise in consumption has been almost entirely of the instant form (about 80 per cent of the total). Most people are still apologetic about the way they make coffee, believing that theirs is surely not the best. Some may walk out from a roaster's shop, too embarrassed to ask for advice. They can certainly derive no inspiration from the miserable brew served up in our public places. In this, our standard is way behind America and we are rightly derided by our European neighbours who are appalled by the invariably weak, too-milky, bitter or stale drink they are served.

I am thankful to say there are signs that things are changing. The making of good real coffee is now the pleasure of a small but growing public. The coffee trade is delighted that more people are flocking to the counters of small specialist shops, and snapping up the ready-ground vacuum-packed branded merchandise from the supermarket shelves. However, although the coffee men are happy that we are drinking more coffee, they only want us to drink more of the same kind. They will not point out the special virtues of Coatepec Mexican, Kona from Hawaii and Mandheling from Sumatra, if it means carrying a larger selection and more trouble in buying. It is also easier to mass produce, distribute and advertise one blend rather than to offer a selection. I hope that this book will in some degree contribute to the reinstatement of coffee, and help give it the attention and respect it deserves.

Few beverages are as intoxicating, heartwarming and utterly satisfying as a steaming cup of hot, freshly made coffee. There is the flavour, the stimulation and the colour, there is body and 'point' (sharpness), and above all there is the aroma. What fragrance is to a rose, aroma is to a cup of coffee. Preserving the fragrance and the fleeting aroma is what good coffee is about, and the secret, as all the pundits often repeat, lies in the word 'fresh'; freshly roasted, freshly ground, freshly made.

The purpose of this book is to help the reader to make the most of what the drink has to offer, and to reveal the infinite possibilities of the virtually untapped area of gastronomic pleasure which is coffee. There are more than a hundred different kinds of coffee, each with its special characteristics. There are various ways of making the drink, each resulting in a slightly different brew, and there are different degrees of roasting and grinding. The lore of coffee is as fascinating as the lore of wine.

I have allowed myself to introduce early legends of exotic beginnings and brief moments of social history, as well as some aspects of the coffee trade, but I have done this only as an enthusiastic amateur. For those who wish to have more expert information on the subject, I should like to refer them to a work by William H. Ukers, former editor of the *Tea and Coffee Trade Journal*. His book *All About Coffee* published in New York in 1922 by this journal, has been my constant companion throughout my research. It is the most complete and authoritative work on the subject compiled for the coffee trade. It is now out of print and naturally to some extent out of date. It can, however, be found in reference libraries and most coffee men usually treasure a copy.

A Tumultuous Start

Coffee is only three centuries old for us in the West, and not one bean was made to germinate outside Africa and Arabia before the seventeenth century. Then, coming from the Levant and arriving first in Venice, it swept tumultuously through the towns of Europe and into America, changing the style of life as it went. The propagation of the plant followed in each country's European colonies in what was often a series of chance adventures.

It acquired its name from the Arabic *qahwah*, through its Turkish form *kahveh* becoming *café* in French, *caffè* in Italian, *koffie* in Dutch and *Kaffee* in German.

Originally a poetic name for wine, the word was transferred towards the end of the thirteenth century in the Yemen to a drink made from the berry of the coffee tree. One explanation for this is that coffee, first inaugurated in Sufi mystic circles, had come to replace the forbidden wine as a drink during religious ceremonies. Delighted by the wakefulness the new drink produced and the help it gave them in their nightly prayers, the early Mohammedans honoured it by giving it the poetic endearment with which they had sung the praise of wine.

Although the earliest written mention of coffee was by Rhazes, an Arabian physician in the tenth century, cultivation may have begun as early as A.D. 575. The coffee tree of the *Coffea arabica* species which gives the best quality coffee is indigenous to Ethiopia, where it grows wild. Other species, such as the *robusta* and the *liberica*, have since been found in other parts of Africa. *Arabica* was first cultivated in the Arabian colony of Harar in Ethiopia. Intensive cultivation came only in the fifteenth century in the Yemen area of South Arabia, from seedlings brought from Ethiopia.

Early legends ascribe the discovery of coffee to various people. The favourite one which has been generally adopted is that of the 'dancing goats'. Kaldi, a young Abyssinian goatherd, used to his sleepy goats, noticed to his amazement that after chewing certain berries they began to prance about excitedly. He tried the berries himself, forgot his troubles, lost his heavy heart and became the happiest person in 'happy Arabia'. A monk from a nearby monastery surprised Kaldi in this state, decided to try the berries too, and invited his brothers to join him. They all felt more alert that night during their prayers. Soon all the monks of the realm were chewing the berries and praying without feeling drowsy.

Another popular tradition of which I am personally fond is related by a certain Hadjiji Khalifa. It concerns Ali bin Omar al-Shadhili, the saint of al-Mukha. Charged with misconduct with the king's daughter who was staying with him for a cure, he was banished into the mountains of Wusab in the Yemen. He and his disciples who followed him in exile ate the berries and drank the decoction they made from boiling them. Then, it seems, victims of an itch epidemic which plagued the inhabitants of Mukha came to him and were cured by taking his coffee. This won him an honourable return and gave him the position of patron saint of coffee growers, coffee-house keepers and coffee drinkers. In Algeria, coffee is also known as 'shadhiliye' after him.

Coffee berries were eaten whole at first, or crushed and mixed with fat. Later, a kind of wine was made with the fermented pulp. In about A.D. 1000 a decoction was made of the dried fruit, beans, hull and all. The practice of roasting the beans was started around the thirteenth century. The drink became popular with dervishes and spread to Mecca and Medina. By the end of the fifteenth century it was passed on by Muslim pilgrims to all parts of the Islamic world, as far as Persia, Egypt, Turkey and North Africa, providing Arabia with a most profitable trade.

Houses of the wealthy had a special room used only for drinking coffee, and servants employed solely to make it. Coffee houses sprang up everywhere people congregated. The more they frequented the coffee houses, the less they went to the mosques. Backgammon, mankala, dancing, music and singing, activities frowned on by the stricter adherents of Islam, also went on in the coffee houses. Having made a start within religion, coffee became a threat to religious observance. The pious tried to prohibit it by invoking the law proscribing wine-drinking.

The establishment, too, was afraid of the joy of life and sense of freedom liberated in the coffee drinkers. Coffee became a subversive drink, gathering people together and sharpening their wits, encouraging political arguments and revolt—a characteristic which was to follow it into Europe and which was felt particularly in times of social unrest. Coffee houses were to be charged again and again with immorality and vice, whether in Cairo, Mecca or Constantinople. At the instigation of religious fanatics or at the whim of a Bey, a Pasha or Kadi (but also once for the sake of a favourite courtesan) they were mobbed and wrecked.

Of the sporadic persecution of coffee houses and drinkers, the most remarkable as well as the most savage was in 1656 when the Ottoman Grand Vizir Koprili suppressed the coffee houses for political reasons, and prohibited coffee. For a first violation the punishment was cudgelling. For a second, the offender was put into a leather bag, which was sewn up and thrown into the Bosphorus. The straits thus claimed many a man.

The introduction of coffee into Europe was not without pitfalls. The more avid its adoption and the wider it spread, the more hostility it aroused. A *Women's Petition Against Coffee* was published in London in 1674, complaining that men were never to be found at home during times of domestic crisis since they were always in the coffee houses, and that the drink rendered them impotent. The following year, in France, attempts were made to discredit the drink, which was seen as an unwelcome competitor by the wine merchants.

In Italy it was the priests who appealed to Pope Clement VIII to have the use of coffee forbidden among Christians. Satan, they said, had forbidden his followers, the infidel Moslems, the use of wine because it was used in the Holy Communion, and given them instead his 'hellish black brew'. It seems the Pope liked the drink, for his reply was: 'Why, this Satan's drink is so delicious that it would be a pity to let the infidels have exclusive use of it.

We shall cheat Satan by baptizing it.' Thus coffee was declared a truly Christian beverage by a farsighted Pope. However, this did not stop the Council of Ten in Venice from trying to eradicate the 'social cankers', the *caffès*, which they charged with immorality, vice and corruption.

Coffee also met with opposition in Sweden, Prussia and Hanover. Frederick the Great, annoyed with the great sums of money going to foreign coffee merchants, issued the following declaration in 1777:

> 'It is disgusting to note the increase in the quantity of coffee used by my subjects and the amount of money that goes out of the country in consequence. Everybody is using coffee. If possible this must be prevented. My people must drink beer. His Majesty was brought up on beer, and so were his officers. Many battles have been fought and won by soldiers nourished on beer; and the King does not believe that coffee-drinking soldiers can be depended upon to endure hardships or to beat his enemies in case of the occurrence of another war.'

It must be said that with all the official sanctions and taxation and the threats of disease and persecution, prohibitions were always more honoured in the breach than in the observance. In fact, coffee gained a greater impetus from the notoriety, and coffee houses survived every effort to suppress them.

Coffee Houses

Although their history has not been smooth, various styles of coffee houses have developed throughout the world for the specific purpose of drinking this privileged brew. We have the leisurely

Continental sidewalk cafés and the *cafés concerts* for the family outing. There are the German *Kaffeeklatsch* ('coffee and gossip') gardens where people bring their own cakes and sandwiches, and the American coffee bars where customers have only a few minutes to snatch a cup of coffee sitting on a high stool.

A certain flavour and style are common to most. Inaugurated in the Levant, they captured the leisure and tranquillity of the local way of life. Coffee houses encourage the convivial spirit. People go there to chat and gossip and be entertained, and sometimes they go to read the newspaper and to play chess or backgammon. In most parts, especially around the Mediterranean, they are not pressed to order nor hurried to leave.

Catering equally for the working and the leisured classes, they have tended to be democratic in character. As a French periodical of the 1850s entitled *Le Café* pointed out in its slogan: 'The *salon* stood for privilege, the café stands for equality.' Coffee has been called the intellectual drink of democracy. In times of upheaval, coffee houses became revolutionary centres, encouraging the interchange of ideas and usually generating liberal and radical opinion. It has been said that the French Revolution was fomented in coffee-house meetings, and the Café Foy was the starting point of its mob spirit.

However, the democratic record has not always been sustained. Women were effectively and undemocratically barred from all coffee houses in England, and in the early days of coffee in Germany the drink was reserved by royal decree for the elect alone. In 1781 Frederick the Great forbade the roasting of coffee except in the courts and royal establishments. He made exceptions in the case of the nobility and of the clergy, of some government officials and his own officers. The *crème de la crème* were obliged to purchase the coffee at high prices directly from the state, but the common people had all their applications for coffee-roasting licences refused. Those who managed to obtain some beans and roasted them illegally were found out by 'coffee smellers'—spies paid to roam the streets in search of revealing smells coming out of windows—and heavily fined.

While coffee drinking has been linked with agitations for

greater freedom, ironically, its production in the Dutch East
Indies, the West Indies, Brazil and most other parts was depen-
dent on the work of slaves or forced labour, and was the result of
colonial exploitation.

The character of each coffee house has naturally reflected that of
its frequenters. Kasters Niebuhr writes about early Syrian coffee
houses in 'Descriptions of Arabia' (Amsterdam, 1774):

> 'Being the only theatres for the exercise of profane eloquence,
> poor scholars attend here to amuse the people. Select portions are
> read, e.g. the adventures of Rustan Sal, a Persian hero. Some
> aspire to the praise of invention, and compose tales and fables.
> They walk up and down as they recite, or assuming oratorial
> consequence, harangue upon subjects chosen by themselves.
>
> 'In one coffee house at Damascus an orator was regularly hired
> to tell his stories at a fixed hour; in other cases he was more
> directly dependent upon the taste of his hearers, as at the con-
> clusion of his discourse, whether it had consisted of literary
> topics or of loose idle tales, he looked to the audience for a
> voluntary contribution.'

The wife of Shah Abbas appointed a *mullah* to sit every day in
the more turbulent establishments of Isfahan in Persia. His job
was to entertain all day with points of law, history and poetry.
Seated high in an ornate chair, he would also tell jokes, sing and
recount the romantic and nostalgic stories of famous lovers or the
Arabian Nights. Thus political hotheads were ignored and con-
troversial issues avoided. Coffee-house storytellers are becoming
fashionable again in Iran today, though sometimes it is the
ubiquitous television that has taken over the role on the raised
chair.

Anyone who has been to Italy knows how much the *caffè* is part
of the good life. The people that frequent them are little different
from those who could be seen around the piazza in Carlo Goldoni's
play *La Bottega di Caffè* (1750), though at this time coffee houses
often also functioned as barbers' shops and gambling houses.

Venetian coffee was said to surpass all others and the Café
Florian's was said to be the best in Venice. Perhaps the most

celebrated coffee house in the world, Florian was opened by
Floriano Francesconi in 1720, by which time all the shops in the
Piazza San Marco had already established themselves as coffee
houses with chairs spilling out into the centre of the Square,
superseding the lemonade vendors, 'acquacedrataios', who had
previously sold coffee. People from all classes frequented Florian,
mostly to hear the latest gossip, and Signor Floriano helped in the
exchange, for he 'long concentrated in himself a knowledge more
varied and multifarious than that possessed by any individual
before or since'. Today, although waitresses no longer fasten
flowers in the gentlemen's buttonholes, violins still serenade the
ladies.

The first person to sell coffee in Paris, an Armenian called
Pascal, sent young coffee waiters through the streets with coffee
pots and oil heaters, shouting '*Café! Café!*' and offering *petits noirs*.
The French bourgeoisie ignored the drink, preferring wines and
spirits, and left the oriental-style coffee houses to the poorer
classes. However, when the Café Procope was opened by François
Procope in 1689, its spacious elegance, its subtle tapestries and
large gilt mirrors, the marble tables, chandeliers and paintings
made coffee respectable and fashionable.

François Procope started as a *limonadier* with a royal licence to
sell spices, barley water and lemonade; but he gave pride of place
to coffee. Being opposite the Comédie Française, he attracted
actors, authors, dramatists and musicians. Among the many
famous 'hommes de lettres' who were his patrons were Voltaire,
Rousseau, Diderot and Beaumarchais, and during the days of the
Revolution, Marat, Robespierre and Danton. Today it is still a
marvellous café and restaurant, serving fine food at 13 rue de
l'Ancienne Comédie.

By 1843 Paris had become one large café, with 3,000 establishments. The historian Michelet described coffee as 'the great event
which created new customs, and even modified human tempera-
ment'. He ascribed to it the intangible and spontaneous flow of
wit which was characteristic of the time. The French coffee shop
ennobled the ways of its frequenters by inaugurating a reign of
temperance and luring people away from the cabaret.

Today the institution is still one where everything is discussed and where people sharpen their wits in debate. It is especially so at the Mabillon, Les Deux Magots and Café de Flore at the Quartier Latin. Here, as at the Véry, les Trois Provençaux and the Café de Chartres of the Palais Royal, the cafés have gained in prestige and reputation what they might have lost financially from customers who spend too long over a cup of coffee.

Historic cafés are still thriving. The Café de la Paix still attracts people to the boulevard des Capucines, Café Durand brings them to the place de la Madeleine, and Voisin's and Mapinot are for the fashionable of the rue St. Honoré. You should visit Tortoni, Café Riche, Maison Dorée and the Café Anglais in the boulevard des Italiens. And of course in Montmartre there are the Café Madrid and the Chat Noir, where painters used to leave canvases in exchange for food and drink. They have appeared in many an Impressionist work and are often used as galleries. One could go on for ever naming the cafés that have not changed in three centuries.

An old anecdote was told to me of a Viennese coffee house where a man had been occupying a seat for some hours. He got up and asked a neighbour: 'Could you please keep my seat while I nip home for a quick cup of coffee?'

A tourist in Vienna in the early eighteenth century wrote about the town which has been called the 'mother of cafés':

'The city of Vienna is filled with coffee houses, where the novelists or those who busy themselves with newspapers delight to meet, to read the gazettes and discuss their contents. Some of these houses have a better reputation than others because such "zeitung-doctors" (doctors in journalism) gather there to pass most unhesitating judgement on the weightiest events, and to surpass all others in their opinions concerning political matters and considerations. All this wins them such respect that many congregate there because of them, and to enrich their minds with inventions and foolishness which they immediately run through the city to bring to the ears of the said personalities.'

After a battering of two wars, Viennese coffee houses still serve delicious coffee with horns, crescents and doughnuts to their habitués, and their special character has been transported by emigrés all over the world. For this reason, at least, we owe a special debt to Franz George Kolschitsky, interpreter for the Turkish Army in 1683, and patron saint of Viennese coffee lovers. The retreating Turkish armies left behind sacks of green coffee beans when they abandoned the siege of Vienna. Kolschitsky collected the sacks and prepared the beans as the Ottomans had done. He sold cups of coffee from door to door and, when his wartime bravery was rewarded by the municipality with a house, he turned it into a coffee house. It was to be the model for all the Viennese cafés that became world famous, as much for their *mélangés* and *schwarze* coffees and their delicious pastries as for the spirit of a grand epoch.

There was a time when the streets of London were so full of coffee houses that people were sure to find one at every corner, guided by the ubiquitous signs of a Turkish coffee pot or the Sultan's head. If a sign did not catch the eye a person had only to sniff the air for the aroma of roasting coffee. England, in fact, had the first coffee house in Europe. It was opened by a Jew from Turkey, a certain Jacob who, benefiting from Cromwell's generous policy towards his co-religionists, was allowed to settle in England. He opened a coffee house in 1650 at Oxford at the Angel in the parish of St. Peter-in-the-East. The first coffee house in London was opened two years later by one Pasqua Rosée, said to be either Armenian or Greek, or both, who had come to England as a servant. He set up with the help of his master in St. Michael's Alley in Cornhill.

Having heard from travellers and merchants to the East about the 'novelty drink', the English were eager to adopt it. One of the most important upholders of the 'Turkish renegade', as coffee was sometimes called, was Sir Henry Blunt, puritan abstainer and so-called 'father' of the English coffee houses.

The influence of coffee houses was enormous on the political, social, literary and commercial life of the times. They were the stage for political debate, fringe centres of education and the origin of certain newspapers. Insurance houses, merchant banks and the stock exchange began in coffee houses. Everything, it seems, went on in these establishments. Edward Robinson describes them in his excellent *The Early English Coffee House*, first published in 1893 (New edition, Dolphin Press, 1972).

Arriving with Puritan rule, an aid to temperance and antidote to alcoholism, halfway between the open tavern and the club, they were well suited to the social climate of the time. They provided a release from the gloomy strictness, but 'decency was never outraged' and it was 'cheaper far than wine'. You could 'for a penny or two spend two or three hours' and you would come out more sprightly than when you came in.

Their democratic character was much in favour. All classes could meet, and nobody was excluded who 'laid down his penny at the bar', especially if he was of 'amiable disposition and a wit'. That is, everybody apart from women, for women were firmly excluded. Macaulay describes the mixed company at Wills': 'earls in stars and garters, clergymen in cassocks, pert templars, sheepish lads from the Universities, translators and index-makers in ragged coats'.

Some coffee houses were frequented by one particular group and eventually almost 'every rank and profession and every shade of political opinion had its own headquarters'. The Rota coffee house was essentially a debating society for the dissemination of republican ideas. Tillyard's was royalist, as was the Grecian in London, which was the beginning of the Royal Society.

Coffee houses near colleges were called 'penny universities' since there, it was said, a man could 'pick up more useful knowledge than he could if applying himself to his books for a whole month'. The penny was the price of a coffee.

Having flourished during the Commonwealth and survived the Great Fire, coffee houses slipped into a new rôle with the Restoration. They became less democratic, more establishment, for the fashionable, the gay and the rich, reflecting the social and intellectual life and splendour of the time. *The Connoisseur* in 1754 described the Bedford, which was typical of the new Restoration style: 'This coffee house is every night crowded with many parts. Almost everyone you meet is a polite scholar and a wit. Jokes and *bons mots* are echoed from box to box; every branch of literature is critically examined, and the merit of every production of the press or performance of the theatres weighed and determined.'

Certain coffee houses in the city were the general mart of stock jobbers and brokers. One in Sweetings Alley became known as the Stock Exchange coffee house. From some evolved the great Mercantile and Shipping Exchange. A 'coffee man', Edward Lloyd, opened Lloyd's coffee house for seafaring men in Tower Street; here underwriters met over coffee and listened to the gossip of the ships and the sea. Merchants and shipowners came to insure their ships and their cargoes, and slaves were occasionally bought. The Baltic Mercantile and Shipping Exchange started at the Virginia and the Jerusalem.

Goldsmiths' and bankers' clerks would meet at coffee houses to settle payments and do their 'outside business'. In 1682 the Bank of Credit was formed and announced that they were ready to do business in the coffee houses and that 'all persons that are desirous to subscribe may come either to Garaway's, Jonathan's or the Amsterdam within Temple Bar, Peter's Coffee House in Covent Garden, or the Mail Coffee House at Charing Cross, at all of which places books will be ready and persons attend from ten to twelve in the morning and from five to seven in the evening'. A room was rented for the clerks to meet regularly at the Five Bells. They later transferred to the Clearing House. At Tom's, the oldest fire insurance service, called the Hand-in-Hand, was formed; this was later incorporated in the Commercial Union. Even doctors used city coffee houses as consulting rooms.

The gossip of the coffee houses found expression in 'Newsletters', privately commissioned by wealthy individuals or institutions such as the Church. These handwritten contributions gathered from rumour were the most valuable source of information at a time when official newspapers were heavily censored. Coffee houses also offered information as well as a ready circulation for established newspapers such as the *Tatler*, the *Spectator* and the *Guardian*. Some provided a 'brass plate' or an ivory tablet with a pencil attached for their customers to write their remarks. The items of news were collected twice a day while still 'hot' for immediate

entry. At Button's, a box in the shape of a lion's head awaited
contributions for the *Guardian*.

However, the importance of coffee houses was not to last
for ever. Their phenomenal rise was equalled only by their spec-
tacular decline. When the time came they disappeared as quickly
as they had come. They had served their unique social purpose and
were no longer needed. Perhaps the English were unable to lay
aside their traditional reserve for ever, at least without resorting
to a genuinely intoxicating beverage. Not all the 'undesirables'
could be eased out, and people did not like to find at their table 'a
gripping Usurer, and next to him a gallant Furioso, then nigh to
him a Virtuoso . . . a player . . . a Country Clown, some prag-
matic . . . a sly phanatick . . . from all parts of the Earth; Dutch,
Danes, Turks and Jews.' They were warned: 'If there you should
observe a person without previous acquaintance, paying you
extraordinary marks of civility, if he puts in for a share of your
conversation with a pretended air of deference; if he tenders his
assistance, and would be suddenly thought your friend, avoid him
as a pest; for these are the usual baits by which the unwary are
caught.'

By the end of the eighteenth century the coffee houses, of which
there had been thousands, had all disappeared. Most of them had
become select members' clubs. The poor and the less exclusive had
slipped back into their earlier rôle of taverns and chop houses.
One institution was certainly pleased. The British East India
Company, far behind the Dutch and the French in the cultivation
of coffee in the British colonies, was more interested in selling tea.
The British Government, wishing to improve trade with India
and China, was glad of the opportunity to encourage tea drinking.
Tea had already been adopted by the Royal Family and the Court,
and women could at last join the men in the new and fashionable
tea gardens. Tea was also better made.

The 'bitter black drink', as Pepys used to call coffee, was made
in various ways, all equally peculiar. Usually served black, it was
boiled with egg shells and sometimes mixed with mustard or
sugar candy. Some concoctions included 'oatmeal, a pint of ale
or any wine, ginger, honey or sugar to please the taste . . . butter

might be added and any cordial powder or pleasant spice'. No wonder coffee was so easily dismissed from favour. Its popularity lay more in the realm of social history than in that of gastronomy.

The social side of coffee drinking is now firmly rooted in the home, while the coffee bars that mushroomed in the fifties, specializing in exotic décor and appealing to the young, have only been able to survive by providing meals. Public houses have taken over the rôle of the old-style coffee houses as meeting places.

As coffee declined in England, it found new favour in Germany, where for many years it had been an indication of high social status. The new favour came from within the enlightened middle classes and the impetus for the spread of the drink came especially from women. The new burgher class of women recently arrived from country to town, freed from work in the fields, found that the *Kaffeeklatsch* was the ideal place to enjoy their new found freedom and leisure. It is in this arena that they tentatively entered the world of ideas, and discussed Goethe and Beethoven as well as babies and scandal—talk which was termed 'coffee-gossip' by a society which felt threatened by, and perhaps a little jealous of the new feminine liberation.

So popular did the drink become that throughout the nineteenth century Germany was far ahead of the rest of Europe in coffee consumption. Coffee had replaced flour soup and beer for breakfast. It was sipped at meal times and at Sunday afternoon family outings in the spacious cafés that became a lively feature of every German city, as famous for their newspapers and magazines as for their delectable pastries—though it was a London merchant who had opened the first coffee house in Hamburg.

Coffee had come to America with immigration since the early eighteenth century. The first coffee houses were modelled after the London ones, but they were more like taverns and inns, serving liquor and meals as well as coffee, tea and chocolate, and even letting rooms. Less joyous and more puritan in character than their European prototypes, they were more devoted to work and business than to witty, idle talk. Like the London coffee houses they were an important part of the life of the country as gathering places for merchants and businessmen. The more important ones had special meeting rooms. These long rooms, a feature which distinguished coffee houses from taverns, were used for meetings of merchants, colonial magistrates and overseers, and all types of public and private business. Occasionally court trials or auctions were held here, and they were also places of Mercantile Insurance where records were held and ships bought and sold. The Chamber of Commerce held sessions in a New York upper long room.

Men carried on their business at the coffee house and went on to the tavern for fun. Eventually they became purely mercantile buildings, while their social and gastronomic functions were divided between clubs, restaurants and hotels.

At first only 'a drink for the well-to-do, except in sips', coffee languished for a time in America while tea rose in favour. It gained an immense impetus following King George's Stamp Act of 1765, the Tea Tax of 1767 and the resulting boycott of tea which was responsible for making the Americans a nation of coffee drinkers.

It was at the Boston 'Tea Party' of 1773, when the citizens of Boston boarded the British ships waiting in the harbour and threw all the British East India tea cargoes overboard, that coffee was crowned once and for all 'King of the American breakfast table'. It was here, too, that coffee became forever linked for the Americans with the War of Independence, with liberty and democracy.

Poison or Elixir?

In an English newspaper advertisement of 1657, coffee was described as 'having many excellent vertues, closes the Orifice of the Stomack, fortifies the heart within, helpeth Dijestion, quickneth the Spirits, maketh the heart lightsome, is good against Eye-sores, coughs or Colds, Rhumes, Consumptions, Head-ache, Dropsie, Gout, Scurvy, King's Evil and many others'. As for the way to use it, this electuary (medicine mixed with honey) was devised: 'Take equal quantity of Butter and Sallet-Oyl, melt them together but not boyle them; Then stirre them well that they may incorporate together: Then melt therewith three times as much Honey, and stirre it well together. Then add thereunto powder of Turkish cophie to make it a thick electuary.'

Coffee was regarded as a medicine from its very beginning. This prejudice, which must have killed the pleasures to be had, was often reversed, but for motives that were not always related to health. When a thesis was put forward by the physicians of Marseilles in 1679 that 'the vile and worthless foreign novelty ... the fruit of a tree discovered by goats and camels ... burned up the blood ... induced palsies, impotence and leanness ... hurtful to the greater part of the inhabitants of Marseilles', they were, it appears, influenced by the local wine merchants.

Variously described as an 'elixir of life' as well as a poison, controversy has always raged over its effects. Threats, however, usually seem to have fallen on deaf ears, a familiar response being Voltaire's: 'I have been poisoning myself for more than eighty years and I am not yet dead.' Even Bach wrote a 'Coffee Cantata' in 1732, mocking a physicians' campaign to discredit coffee in Germany.

Among various investigations carried out over the years to settle the controversy, a notable one was made in Sweden in the eighteenth century. Identical twin brothers were condemned to death for murder. King Gustav III commuted their sentences to life imprisonment on condition that one twin be given a large daily dose of tea and the other of coffee. The tea drinker died first at the age of 83. The question was settled, and today the Swedish people are amongst the world leaders in coffee consumption.

Today some of the old misconceptions, such as that coffee was a promoter of impotence, barrenness and sterility, have been ex-ploded, but the controversy as to its effects on health is still not resolved. Fortunately the health scare, which has assumed some importance in the U.S.A. and produced a vast increase in the market for decaffeinated coffee, has not taken hold in the United Kingdom. Present research is still inconclusive as to any possible link between coffee consumption and disease, and has failed to eliminate the element of individual and psychological idiosyncrasy. Some people do suffer the ill effects of 'caffeinism': insomnia, irritation, headache, palpitations, fever, weight loss and upset stomach, but nearly always when there has been over-indulgence in the drink.

General opinion is that coffee in moderation is not harmful. The limit of moderation is a matter of individual constitution, and that can only be decided from personal experience.

As a food, coffee has not much value since the protein content is insoluble and remains with the grounds. But it aids digestion and acts as a diuretic, and of course it offers stimulation. It is the stimulating constituent caffeine which acts on the nervous system and on muscles, increasing mental activity and heightening perception without any subsequent depression. And it is this property, either real or psychological, which causes some people to be robbed of sleep if they drink coffee too near their bedtime. A paradox is that the late evening cup of tea which often replaces it also contains caffeine, though to a smaller degree. Cocoa, chocolate and Coca-Cola also contain it.

However, I have not been alone in noticing that a good meal preceding coffee mitigates the effect of caffeine, and that coffee containing milk or cream is not as stimulating as black coffee. Indeed, I have even heard that while black coffee has kept some people awake, coffee with cream makes them drowsy. In a high or continental roast some of the caffeine has been sublimed off by roasting, which might explain why Continentals and people from the Middle East are less worried about caffeine than Americans, who prefer lighter roasts. Although caffeine is considered by some to be a drug as addictive as nicotine, it is difficult to think of drinking coffee as an addiction, so much is it part of everyday life. If a habit is formed, it is not necessarily detrimental or injurious, and the desire for the drink can be easily broken.

Different beans contain different amounts of caffeine. As a

general rule, the better the quality, the less the caffeine, and Robustas which make up the bulk of the instant coffees contain the most. Some species of coffee trees produce caffeine-free beans, but these have, unfortunately, such an unpleasant flavour that they are not commercially used.

Meanwhile, for the benefit of the caffeine-sensitive and the caffeine-conscious, caffeine (which is so soluble in hot water that all methods of brewing fully extract it) has been removed to a great degree from many types of beans by extracting it with solvents. This can be more easily done with grounds than with whole beans. Usually the green beans are softened by steam and water, flushed with a solvent containing chlorine which combines with the caffeine, then heated and blown with steam to remove all traces of the solvent. The taste inevitably suffers: in some of the worst of the decaffeinated coffees, much of the aromatic and flavouring constituents have also disappeared with the caffeine, and even the best never have the wonderful flavour of the real thing.

Many quips and sallies written from when coffee was new in France by such men as Hugo, Flaubert, Baudelaire, Balzac and Zola, testify to its power to stimulate creative work without unpleasant side effects.

Prince Talleyrand (1754–1839) expressed a general feeling when he said about a cup of coffee that it 'detracts nothing from your intellect; on the contrary, your stomach is freed by it and no longer distresses your brain; it will not hamper your mind with troubles but give freedom to its working. Suave molecules of Mocha stir up your blood, without causing excessive heat; the organ of thought receives from it a feeling of sympathy; work becomes easier and you will sit down without distress to your principal repast which will restore your body and afford you a calm delicious night.'

To most of us the stimulation of coffee is one of its great attractions. It is certainly to the much maligned caffeine that it owes its survival through generations of hamfisted methods of preparation that destroyed most of its enjoyment as a drink in its own right.

Custom and Ritual

Few travellers to the Levant fail to notice the luxury of tranquil enjoyment possessed by those who sit in front of a tiny cup filled with syrupy, frothy, black coffee, epitome of a way of life which prizes 'kayf' (peace of mind) above all things. They may sit in the silent darkness of a cavern-like shop, a *narghileh* (water pipe) passing from one to the other, or in an open-air café spilling across the street, surrounded by the animated shouts of 'Shish! Bish!' of backgammon players and the clapping of their dice and counters. Sometimes two chairs alone, one acting as armrest, footstool and table, outside a barber's shop, invite them to the moment of bliss. Certainly the Arab dictum: 'As with art 'tis prepared, so one should drink it with art', is honoured in this part of the world where coffee was first made.

Perhaps it is the early religious use of coffee that has given it a ceremonial character in the world of Islam. The dervishes of old drank coffee to keep awake during the nights given to religious devotion. The drink was kept warm in a large red earthenware vessel, each dervish receiving some in turn from his superior, who dipped their small bowls into the jar. They sipped the coffee while they chanted 'Allah w' akbar!' (God is great). After the dervishes were served, the jar was passed round to the rest of the congregation. Never was a religious ceremony performed without coffee being drunk.

Today, centuries after it became secularized, coffee drinking is still in the Middle East an activity enmeshed in ritual, practised at all times throughout the day.

An ancient Arab coffee ceremony is beautifully described by Palgrave in Uker's *All About Coffee*:

'The K'hāwah was a large oblong hall, about twenty feet in height, fifty in length, and sixteen, or thereabouts, in breadth; the walls were coloured in a rudely decorative manner with brown and white wash, and sunk here and there into small triangular recesses, destined to the reception of books, though of these Ghafil at least had no over-abundance, lamps, and other such like objects. The roof of timber, and flat; the floor was strewed with fine clean sand, and garnished all round alongside of the walls with long strips of carpet, upon which cushions, covered with faded silk, were disposed at suitable intervals. In poorer houses felt rugs usually take the place of carpets.

'In one corner, namely, that furthest removed from the door, stood a small fireplace, or, to speak more exactly, furnace, formed of a large square block of granite, or some other hard stone, about twenty inches each way; this is hollowed inwardly into a deep funnel, open above, and communicating below with a small horizontal tube or pipe-hole, through which the air passes, bellows-driven, to the lighted charcoal piled up on a grating about half-way inside the cone. In this manner the fuel is soon brought to a white heat, and the water in the coffee-pot placed upon the funnel's mouth is readily brought to boil. The system of coffee furnaces is universal in Djowf and Djebel Shomer, but in Nejed itself, and indeed in whatever other yet more distant regions of Arabia I visited to the south and east, the furnace is replaced by an open fireplace hollowed in the ground floor, with a raised stone border, and dog-irons for the fuel, and so forth, like what may be yet seen in Spain. This diversity of arrangement, so far as Arabia is concerned, is due to the greater abundance of fire-wood in the south, whereby the inhabitants are enabled to light up on a larger scale; whereas throughout the Djowf and Djebel Shomer wood is very scarce, and the only fuel at hand is bad charcoal, often brought from a considerable distance, and carefully husbanded.

'This corner of the K'hāwah is also the place of distinction whence honour and coffee radiate by progressive degrees round the apartment, and hereabouts accordingly sits the master of the house himself, or the guests whom he more especially delightes to honour.

'On the broad edge of the furnace or fireplace, as the case may be, stands an ostentatious range of copper coffee-pots, varying in size and form. Here in the Djowf their make resembles that in vogue at Damascus; but in Nejed and the eastern districts they are of a different and much more ornamental fashioning, very tall and slender, with several ornamental circles and mouldings in elegant relief, besides boasting long beak-shaped spouts and high steeples for covers. The number of these utensils is often extravagantly great. I have seen a dozen at a time in a row by one fireside, though coffee-making requires, in fact, only three at most. Here in the Djowf five or six are considered to be the thing; for the south this number must be doubled; all this to indicate the riches and munificence of their owner, by imply-ing the frequency of his guests and the large amount of coffee that he is in consequence obliged to have made for them.

'Behind this stove sits, at least in wealthy houses, a black slave, whose name is generally a diminutive in token of familiarity or affection; in the present case it was Soweylim, the diminutive of Sālim. His occupation is to make and pour out the coffee; where there is no slave in the family, the master of the premises himself, or perhaps one of his sons, performs that hospitable duty; rather a tedious one, as we shall soon see.

'We enter. On passing the threshold it is proper to say, "*Bismillah*," i.e., "in the name of God;" not to do so would be looked on as a bad augury alike for him who enters and for those within. The visitor next advances in silence, till on coming about half-way across the room, he gives to all present, but looking specially at the master of the house, the customary "*Es-salamu'aleykum*," or "Peace be with you," literally, "on you." All this while every one else in the room has kept his place, motionless, and without saying a word. But on receiving the salaam of etiquette, the master of the house rises, and if a strict Wahhābee, or at any rate desirous of seeming such, replies with the full-length traditionary formula. "*W' 'aleykumu-s-salāmu, w'rahmat' Ullahi w'barakátuh*," which is, as every one knows,

"And with (or, on) you be peace, and the mercy of God, and his blessings." But should he happen to be of anti-Wahhābee tendencies the odds are that he will say *"Marhaba,"* or *"Ahlan w' sahlan,"* i.e., "welcome" or "worthy, and pleasurable," or the like; for of such phrases there is an infinite, but elegant, variety.

'All present follow the example thus given, by rising and saluting. The guest then goes up to the master of the house, who has also made a step or two forwards, and places his open hand in the palm of his host's, but without grasping or shaking, which would hardly pass for decorous, and at the same time each repeats once more his greeting, followed by the set phrases of polite enquiry, "How are you?" "How goes the world with you?" and so forth, all in a tone of great interest, and to be gone over three or four times, till one or other has the discretion to say *"El hamdu l'illāh,"* "Praise be to God", or, in equivalent value, "all right," and this is a signal for a seasonable diversion to the ceremonious interrogatory.

'The guest then, after a little contest of courtesy, takes his seat in the honoured post by the fireplace, after an apologetical salutation to the black slave on the one side, and to his nearest neighbour on the other. The best cushions and newest looking carpets have been of course prepared for his honoured weight. Shoes or sandals, for in truth the latter alone are used in Arabia, are slipped off on the sand just before reaching the carpet, and they remain on the floor close by. But the riding stick or wand, the inseparable companion of every true Arab, whether Bedouin or townsman, rich or poor, gentle or simple, is to be retained in the hand, and will serve for playing with during the pauses of conversation, like the fan of our great-grandmothers in their days of conquest.

'Without delay Soweylim begins his preparations for coffee. These open by about five minutes of blowing with the bellows and arranging the charcoal till a sufficient heat has been produced. Next he places the largest of the coffee-pots, a huge machine, and about two-thirds full of clear water, close by the edge of the glowing coal-pit, that its contents may become gradually warm while other operations are in progress. He then

takes a dirty knotted rag out of a niche in the wall close by
and having untied it, empties out of it three or four handfuls of
unroasted coffee, the which he places on a little trencher of
platted grass, and picks carefully out any blackened grains, or
other non-homologous substances, commonly to be found inter-
mixed with the berries when purchased in gross; then, after
much cleansing and shaking, he pours the grain so cleansed into
a large open iron ladle, and places it over the mouth of the funnel,
at the same time blowing the bellows and stirring the grains
gently round and round till they crackle, redden, and smoke a
little, but carefully withdrawing them from the heat long before
they turn black or charred, after the erroneous fashion of
Turkey and Europe; after which he puts them to cool a moment
on the grass platter.

'He then sets the warm water in the large coffee-pot over the
fire aperture, that it may be ready boiling at the right moment, and
draws in close between his own trouserless legs a large stone
mortar, with a narrow pit in the middle, just enough to admit
the large stone pestle of a foot long and an inch and a half thick,
which he now takes in hand. Next, pouring the half-roasted
berries into the mortar, he proceeds to pound them, striking
right into the narrow hollow with wonderful dexterity, nor ever
missing his blow till the beans are smashed, but not reduced
into powder. He then scoops them out, now reduced to a sort
of coarse reddish grit, very unlike the fine charcoal dust which
passes in some countries for coffee, and out of which every
particle of real aroma has long since been burnt or ground.

'After all these operations, each performed with as intense a
seriousness and deliberate nicety as if the welfare of the entire
Djowf depended on it, he takes a smaller coffee-pot in hand, fills
it more than half with hot water from the larger vessel, and
then shaking the pounded coffee into it, sets it on the fire to
boil, occasionally stirring it with a small stick as the water rises
to check the ebullition and prevent overflowing. Nor is the
boiling stage to be long or vehement; on the contrary, it is and
should be as light as possible. In the interim he takes out of
another rag-knot a few aromatic seeds called heyl, an Indian

product, but of whose scientific name I regret to be wholly ignorant, or a little saffron, and after slightly pounding these ingredients, throws them into the simmering coffee to improve its flavour, for such an additional spicing is held indispensable in Arabia though often omitted elsewhere in the East. Sugar would be a totally unheard of profanation. Last of all, he strains off the liquor through some fibres of the inner palm-bark placed for that purpose in the jug-spout, and gets ready the tray of delicate parti-coloured grass, and the small coffee cups ready for pouring out. All these preliminaries have taken up a good half-hour.'

Although the stringent rules of etiquette are no longer carried to such extremes, and the ritual is never now quite so elaborate, oriental customs surrounding coffee have not changed very much.

In Arabia a watered down form of an early coffee drinking ceremony still exists, starting with a string of gestures, greetings, praises to God, enquiries into health, traditional formulas of courtesy of an infinite and elegant variety. Rules of etiquette are observed in serving, in some cases involving each process of making, each performed with intense seriousness and deliberate nicety. The tiny, half-egg-sized cups are refilled three or four times. To refuse is an unforgivable insult.

In this proverbially hospitable area, coffee is the symbol of hospitality. It is considered an outrage not to offer a cup of coffee to anyone who enters your house and an almost equal outrage to refuse. Coffee is made individually as soon as a visitor arrives, always freshly brewed in the small, long-handled copper or brass pots called *kanaka* or *ibrik*, sometimes roasted and pounded just before brewing. Tiny cups are set out on inlaid brass trays, as well as several glasses of water, sometimes scented with rosewater, to be drunk before, not after, so as not to wash down the taste of coffee. A bowl of jam may be set with little spoons hung on the side for guests to relish a little at a time as they take their coffee. On special occasions a few small pastries are piled on an elegant little plate. It is essential that each cup of coffee must have its share of the foam, which is called *wesh* (face). To ensure this, coffee is poured with a slight quiver of the hand. An important person is served first, the oldest next, and women last. Among Bedouins, cups are served only half filled. A filled one would mean: 'Drink up and go!'—a bitter insult also shown in the adage: 'Fill the cup for your enemy'. Here ritual insists that the pourer should be served first to ensure that the pot is not a deadly one for the person of most importance who is served next. It is not unknown for people to have been dispatched to another world with poison slipped into a cup of coffee. At this stage comes a great deal of arguing with shouts of 'Abadan! Abadan!' as each guest refuses, wishing to honour his neighbour more.

Since sugar is boiled at the same time as the coffee, guests are always asked their preference—whether they would like it sweet (*belou* or *sukar ziada*), medium (*mazbout*) or unsweetened (*murra*)— and they are served accordingly. The sweetness of the drink is sometimes determined by the occasion. At a happy one, such as a wedding or a birthday, it is served sweet, while at a funeral it must be drunk without any sugar at all.

In Turkey at one time, a man promised when he married never to let his wife go without coffee, and it was considered a legitimate cause for divorce if he neglected to do so. So important is coffee in Oriental life that it is common for beggars to ask for money to buy it. It is inconceivable that they should go without. Business and bargaining are always done over a cup of coffee served before the argument starts. Whether in a shop or a market stall it creates a bond and an obligation between buyer and seller. Some people drink up to twenty-five cups a day, but these are so small, sometimes thimble-sized, that they do not amount to too much.

The habit of the coffee house is one that has required a certain leisure. Ceremony, too, has been required in the coffee houses of the Levant, where customers often sip their water and smoke a *narghileh* (water pipe) while waiting – for the service takes time. Only men go to the resorts of the 'lower orders'. Some bring their own pipe and tobacco, and sometimes hashish. The coffee-shop owner keeps two or three *narghilehs* which are used for both tobacco and hashish. Customers have to wait their turn. Etiquette prevails. A newcomer salutes each person on entering a crowded coffee room and is saluted in return. In the past it was usual for the entire company to rise when an old man entered and to yield him the inside corner chair. Such courtesies take time, and one sometimes has to wait for the beans to be roasted and milled.

In early Arabia, Burckhardt relates that respectable people were never seen in a coffee shop, but they were always filled with the lower classes and seafarers. An Arab who could not afford to ask a friend to dine would invite him in from the coffee shop when he saw him pass, and would be highly offended if the invitation was rejected. The waiter, in presenting the coffee to the guest would cry aloud for all to hear: 'Jabba!' (gratis).

These ways have been spread by the Ottomans throughout their old Empire around the Mediterranean shores. Today in Cyprus a man sitting in a coffee shop will call to passers-by 'Kopiaste', inviting them to join him. If you happen to be in a strange village and sit in a coffee shop, you will probably find that your coffee has been paid for by someone else.

As children, we were usually afraid of the scenes that occurred when the heads of families, enjoying a coffee and a cake together, fought to pay everyone's bill. It is still the greatest honour to be the host.

Very little of the oriental ceremony has been retained on our Western breakfast tables, but our casual entertaining is still over a cup of coffee and a degree of ritual is needed if it is to be properly made. The care we take in serving, be it in hand-warming bowls or elegant cups accompanied by coffee cakes, and the little rituals and courtesies of coffee time may not change its virtues, but they do add to its enjoyment.

Three Hundred Years of Trade

An Italian wrote from Constantinople in 1615:

'The Turks have a drink of black colour, which during the summer is very cooling, whereas in the winter it heats and warms the body, remaining always the same beverage and not changing its substance. They swallow it hot as it comes from the fire and they drink it in long draughts, not at dinner time, but as a kind of dainty and sipped slowly while talking with one's friends. One cannot find any meetings among them where they drink it not. . . . With this drink which they call "cahue", they divert themselves in their conversations. . . . When I return I will bring some with me and I will impart the knowledge to the Italians.'

Many European travellers to the Levant were already reporting on the strange drink.

In the same year Venetian merchants brought coffee beans into Europe from Moka, five years after the Dutch brought tea, and eighty years after cocoa was introduced by the Spanish.

This was the start of a most lucrative trade for the Arabians, one they jealously guarded for a hundred years while they were the sole providers of coffee to the world. Berries were not allowed out of the country without first being steeped in boiling water or parched to destroy their power of germination and strangers were prohibited from visiting plantations—a difficult task with so many pilgrims journeying to Mecca. It was in fact a pilgrim from India who smuggled out the first beans capable of germination.

The first coffee plant to be brought to Europe was stolen by Dutch traders in 1616. The Netherlands East India Company realized the commercial advantages of cultivating the bean and by the end of the century they had set up plantations in the Dutch colonies of Ceylon, Java and Sumatra, Celebes, Timor and Bali.

The French followed in a less businesslike, more romantic way with the introduction of coffee into their own colonies. A coffee plant was presented to Louis XIV by the burgomaster of Amsterdam in 1714. It blossomed in the Jardin des Plantes, tended by the royal botanist, Antoine de Jussieu. It was destined, through the initiative of a young naval officer from Normandy, Gabriel Mathieu de Clieu, to become the progenitor of all the coffees of the Caribbean and the Americas. Delighted by the drink he discovered in the Paris coffee houses during a visit from Martinique, and hearing about the plantations in Java, he became obsessed with the idea of starting cultivation in the French colonies.

Having obtained a seedling through clever intrigue, he set sail for Martinique with the tender young plant in a glass box. The voyage was fraught with misadventure and the plant in constant danger, not least from a passenger who repeatedly tried to destroy it and even managed to tear off some leaves during a struggle with de Clieu. Surviving a fierce tempest and flooding with salt water as well as a period of water rationing during which it shared de Clieu's own scant supply, the seedling was eventually planted in the officer's garden in Martinique, surrounded by thorny bushes and under constant surveillance of an armed guard. This tiny plant was to provide all the rich estates of the West Indies and Latin America.

Coffee was introduced soon after in Spain's West Indian Colonies of Puerto Rico and Cuba.

Britain was the last country to cultivate coffee in its colonies. It started cultivation in Jamaica in 1730 and waited till 1840 to begin cultivation in India, where it had previously concentrated on tea.

At the same time Brazil entered the field, acquiring the plant, as legend relates, through the charms of a lieutenant colonel Francisco de Melo Palheta. The Brazilian officer, having attracted the attentions of the Governor's wife on a visit to French Guiana in 1727, received a coffee plant hidden in a bouquet of flowers as a token of her affection. This gift was the start of the greatest coffee empire in the world. Progress was slow at first, with Roman Catholic missionaries playing a major part in spreading coffee growing throughout Brazil and in other parts of South America.

In the middle of the nineteenth century, the terrible leaf disease *Hemileia vastatrix* struck Asia. Within a few years it had completely wiped out coffee in India and Ceylon, Java, Sumatra and Malaya, leaving the field wide open to Brazil with its ideal volcanic soil, its moist foggy climate and its large slave labour force.

By the end of the century Brazil had achieved supremacy in world coffee production, a position it still holds today. The mass consumption of coffee had spread throughout the world, and coffee had entered its golden age. It is Brazil's growing and enormous production that has changed the role of coffee from luxury drink to common everyday beverage. Its problem soon became one of over-planting and over-production, while in Colombia, it was a matter of overcoming the difficulties of growing and transportation on the high slopes of the Andes.

So large and dependable has the world consumer demand become, with America in the lead, that to satisfy it a coffee growing belt has spread to all lands of suitable climate across the world. Lying between the tropic of Cancer and the tropic of Capricorn, the belt spreads thickly across the Americas, through the islands of the Caribbean and the now turbulent areas of Africa and Arabia. It embraces the Malgasy Republic, India and the East Indian and Pacific Islands. In more than 60 countries, it provides a living for some 25 million people and gives the beans a most important part in world trade as a commodity second only to oil.

Since the Second World War the main feature of world coffee production and commerce has been the enormous rise in importance of the African countries as coffee suppliers. Their contribution has been mainly in the cheaper coffees in competition with Brazil.

Brazil, however, with Colombia a close second, still dominates the coffee markets of the world. While Yemen, the first producer, slips into inactivity, some of the old coffee producing countries are active again and new countries are making inroads into the South American supremacy.

Despite its success, the history of coffee production has been the chequered one of a delicate tropical crop threatened by the vagaries of weather, disease and natural disaster. With the growing fierce competition of the last decades, it has also been one of recurring cycles of over-production and under-production with the accompanying price changes. Merchandizing had developed into a ruthless free-for-all, with price cutting and dumping and burning of mountains of unsaleable coffee (as in Brazil) for many years.

Merchants are to some extent protected against price changes in the London 'futures' market by buying and selling in advance. The Coffee Terminal Market Association acts mostly as an international insurance market, interpreting world conditions and anticipating supply and demand trends. Speculation, however, also results in artificial price rises.

Trading for the cheaper *robusta* coffees alone is carried on at the London Commodity Exchange, Plantation House. *Arabicas* and Milds are traditionally sold straight to the buyers, as are the Brazils, which are government controlled.

For the growers it is more serious. The economies of the larger coffee producing nations lie precariously on the fortunes of the coffee crop, as does the livelihood of the coffee farmers. National Federations have attempted to stabilize prices at the highest possible level by regulating planting and buying up any surplus so that over-production does not force prices down.

The International Coffee Organisation of producing and consumer countries was formed in London in 1962 in an effort to stabilize the world coffee trade to benefit both producer and consumer. For ten years it controlled export quotas and therefore production, though it had no power to control the price of coffees which are sold directly or by auction on the open market. With obvious conflicts of interest, growing dissension on quotas, selectivity and readjustment systems and criticism that prices were kept down for the consuming countries, the International Coffee Agreement lapsed in 1973.

The coffee producing countries alone have now formed international corporations, intending, by decreasing supplies, to force prices as high as they can.

The devastating Black Frost, which crippled millions of trees in Brazil on the night of 17th July 1975, was the immediate reason for the latest price rises. The 'price' coffees are also suffering scarcity. Political unrest in many African countries has contributed with Brazil's crop tragedy to a new, though temporary, world shortage.

Inevitably, the day of cheap coffee is gone forever. Prices will most certainly remain high. They have been too low for too long, especially for the quality growths relying as they do on intensive and increasingly costly hand labour. If margins of profit are not maintained at a reasonably high level, it is conceivable that growers may switch to more profitable and more nutritive crops such as soya beans and wheat, which also require less care.

Whatever the future market trends, the Abyssinian goatherd's discovery is here to stay. It has already gone a long way, thanks to Hadjiji Khalifa and Baba Budan, to Kolchitsky, de Clieu and Francisco de Melo Palheta. Coffee owes its success to the special care of farmers, pickers and processors, and to the affectionate skill of roasters; but it is the rich nutrients of the soil, the right sloping of mountainsides and the soft caresses of the sun and rain that have given us the infinite variety of tastes and aromas which is one of the treasures of our civilization.

The Coffee Tree

One of the peculiarities of the coffee tree is that the fruit ripens several times a year. Another is that it bears at the same time both blossom and berries (also called cherries) at various stages of maturity. The entire style of the coffee trade is governed by this caprice of nature. If the cherries are allowed to grow overripe, the beans inside are spoilt. If they are unripe, the beans will not ripen once picked. So pickers of quality coffees must return to the same tree time and time again to pick only the ripe cherries—an inordinate amount of labour for the 2 lb. of clear green beans which is an average yearly yield for one tree. Bear it in mind when you next buy coffee.

There are more economical labour-saving methods of harvesting favoured by the growers of cheaper coffees, but they result in inferior, harsher tasting grades, burdened by impurities. In many parts of Africa, trees are shaken and berries picked from the ground before they are injured or rotten. In the greater part of Brazil, where the lower priced coffees are produced, branches are stripped of everything at once, leaves, flowers, overripe and under-ripe cherries. The mutilated trees take two years to recover from this savage treatment.

A coffee tree is a rare, magnificent sight when it breaks out into a fragile and delicate white blossom, its fragrance as intoxicating as that of the orange and the jasmine which it resembles. It may bloom alone like a young bride or with the whole farm, a swaying sea of white petals, as beautiful as they are ephemeral. For in two or three days they will have fluttered off the bough, leaving their perfume to linger only a while longer.

Soon, tiny clusters of cherries appear, green at first, then yellow, red and deep crimson. When they are almost black, they are ready to pick. In Jamaica, bats are the first to know when the fruit is ripe. Their nightly sucking of the sweet pulp is a signal for the farmers to start harvesting. The oval berries sit in tight bunches hugging the branches from which the long, polished, dark green, lance-shaped leaves sprout in pairs. These are firm, but softer and paler on the underside and scalloped towards the edges. Branches also grow two by two on opposite sides of the trunk.

The evergreen trees are usually grown from seed in nursery beds, and transferred after a year to the plantation ground, in exactly the same way as the Arabs first raised and cultivated the plants. For the first four or five years of its life, the coffee tree is too busy growing roots and building a strong straight trunk and an umbrella of branches to bear a crop of beans. It will usually only produce a full crop in its sixth year and continue until the fifteenth year, when the yield declines. Left to nature it would grow to a height of fourteen to twenty feet and some even to forty feet. Apart from the regions where they are allowed to grow wild, they are generally kept pruned to a height of six feet to make picking easier and to reserve their strength for producing beans.

There are three main species of coffee plants grown commercially, each with its own varieties. *Coffea arabica* is the most important and produces the best quality beans. Found growing wild in Ethiopia, it is also the most widely cultivated. *Liberica* is a native of Liberia, while *robusta* originates in the Congo. As the latter name implies, they are stronger, withstand wider extremes of climate and are less susceptible to disease. They need less care in hoeing, weeding and pruning, and are often allowed to grow wild in forest conditions. Although 'hard' in flavour and of inferior quality to *arabica*, *robusta* has been adopted by the African continent in a big way. Its high yield makes it ideal for instant coffees. While *arabica* flourishes best at high altitudes from 2,000 to 6,500 feet above sea level—the higher the altitude the finer the quality—*liberica* and *robusta* do better below 2,000 feet.

Coffee trees only grow in tropical and sub-tropical lands. Within the limits of the 'coffee belt' they are able to grow in widely different climates, in different soils, at different altitudes and with varying amounts of rainfall. They thrive equally in the hot, humid valleys and rainy forests of Africa, in the cold, windy and foggy highlands of Central America, as well as in the changing weather of drought, torrential rain and stormy winds in the Caribbean. Here lies the reason for the different characteristics of the infinite variety of beans.

Ideal conditions are a temperature ranging between 65 °F. and 75 °F., a good altitude and enough rain (from 40 to 120 inches a year). The time of rainfall is important. Alternating heavy rain and strong sun are needed for maturation, and a dry spell is needed for harvesting. Almost any type of soil will do, but the best is a mixture of disintegrated volcanic rock with an addition of decomposed mould and porous, permeable soil.

Sunshine is needed only a few hours a day. Hilly ground is ideal because it provides for only a short exposure, as well as making for good drainage. Coffee trees do not like their feet wet. Tall leafy trees are planted among the coffee trees as windbreaks and to give shade.

As for the hazards, frost and leaf disease are the usual killers.

Preparing the Beans

Inside the sweet, gummy pulp of the fruit lie the precious green coffee beans. Flat-faced, marked by a thin incision, they hug each other face to face, protected by a tough outer hull, the parchment, and an interior, delicate, semi-transparent covering, the 'silver skin'.

Preparation for market is by removing all these outer layers, and is done by either of two methods. The 'wet' one, for washed coffees, is considered the better and is used for the hand-picked quality growths. The berries acquire a distinctive and attractive taste during thirty hours of steeping in fermentation tanks. The 'dry' method, which gives 'naturals', is more economical and used where water is scarce. Beans are spread out to dry in the sun for three weeks and turned over frequently. Cleaning is not as effective as in the 'wet' method but 'naturals' have the advantage of ageing better.

Beans are then sized, sorted, picked over to remove bad ones and graded, all by hand, with extra care taken for the higher grades. There is probably nothing we use that demands so much in terms of human effort. If value is related to the amount of handling and labour, coffee should indeed be placed high in our esteem.

Choosing Coffee

The Spanish proverb 'Sobre los gustos no hay disputa' (in the matter of taste there is no argument) is appropriate. The best coffee is the one you like best. Coffee is a fleeting moment and fragrance, which, to quote Brillat-Savarin, 'I can no more describe than the perfume of yesterday's violets'. I cannot find the right words, nor give an identity to the sensations each coffee has given me. They have been many, and so too have the memories they stirred. I would far rather put a steaming cup in your hand and say, 'Taste it! Smell it! Look at it!'

The coffee trade, however, has come up with a list of evocative adjectives. The most highly prized tastes are the 'acidy', the 'bitter' (which is not derived from high roasting or boiling) and the 'sweet', which is one of my favourites. There are the 'rich' and the 'mellow' from ageing. There are the 'smooth' and 'velvety', and the 'winy', resulting from a little fermentation. The 'neutral' is far more attractive than its name implies, the 'gamy' is spicy and as exotic as its place of origin.

The lesser tastes do not appear in the specialist shops as single coffees, but find anonymity in the blended brands. Of these, the 'flat' is as dull as it sounds. The 'wild', the 'grassy' or the 'muddy' come from the ground they have fallen on. 'Harshness', 'sourness' and 'hidyness' will be lost in the high roasting and the 'fermented' taste is due to neglect. The area of Rio has given its name to the least palatable taste from Brazil, the 'Rioy'. The least attractive in taste are, however, the most attractive in price and very much in demand for the instant coffee market.

Product of nature, slave to its vagaries, there is an element of mystery in each crop and each shipment even from the same farm. No two beans are the same, even if they are picked from the same branch. Coffee is affected not only by climate, the great variable, by soil and cultivation, but also by styles of picking, processing, storage and transportation.

There being no regularity, predictability and stability in the quality of growths, you can only trust the judgement of your coffee man and hope that he will keep up his standard of quality when he goes to buy again. He will taste and try. He may have to upgrade his habitual purchase or find a cheaper equivalent to one that has priced itself out of the market; or a replacement for one that has become scarce because of a natural disaster or local political problems.

This explains why a Mocha in one shop is often different from the Mocha of another shop, and why a Mocha occasionally fails to live up to its promise. Another reason may be that a merchant does not roast often and that the coffee he sells is stale.

Very few coffees are good enough to be drunk by themselves. There are, of course, the 'self-drinkers', the aristocrats of the trade, which can be drunk straight, but only a few of these are available in this country. And even these single, highly prized growths will usually benefit from marriage with one or more other types. Each type of bean has its special attributes and weaknesses. No single variety of coffee cheap enough and suitable for mass distribution, contains the necessary elements for a drink equal to one achieved by combining different types of coffee. Here lies the reason for blending which seeks to create, by blending various coffees, a single one with a combination of delightful traits—a balanced composition of the best attributes of each.

With the changing components which are the beans, the blender must maintain a standard of quality and consistency. Here lies the art of blending, for it is an art as much in the mass market as in the specialist trade, and the results a closely guarded secret. Seven or eight coffees with complementary characteristics are generally chosen. Acidy, syrupy, and neutral varieties are combined in such a way that flavour, aroma, appearance and price are properly related to produce a smooth drink combining all the better qualities. In general, you are safe in choosing a specialist merchant's 'house blend'. It will probably be good since he stakes his reputation on it, and reasonably priced as he may use some cheaper beans as well.

Naturally the speciality blenders are more likely to achieve the highest standards of taste and quality, while blenders of mass-produced coffees, to reach the widest market at a competitive price, must choose the more abundant, lower priced coffees which are also the less interesting and the more neutral. However, even the specialist merchant's house blend must be pleasing to a broad range of tastes, and therefore a trifle unremarkable. You may like to ask for an additional dark roast or an extra-aromatic growth in the blend.

You may also like to create your own blends.

Try a little experimental blending yourself and find the right blends to suit your taste. Ask your dealer to help you. Talk to him about the qualities you like and dislike in his blends and ask his advice about variations on these until you achieve a perfect balance of flavour, body and aroma. There are the partnerships that tradition has cemented like Mocha and Mysore, the Turkish coffee favourites, high roasted and pulverized, from which you can derive inspiration.

Honoré de Balzac made famous a blend of Brazilian Bourbon, Martinique and Mocha which his servant purchased in three different shops. Martinique is no longer available but can be replaced by Haiti or Cuban.

Other combinations that you might like to try are:

Java and Mocha

Brazilian Bourbon Santos and Colombian Bogota

Colombian Medellin and Ethiopian Mocha

Costa Rican, Java and Mocha

Sumatra and Mocha

Bogota Colombian, washed Venezuelan Maracaibo, Brazilian Santos

Coatepec Mexican, Cobans from Guatemala and Mandheling from Java

Kenya, Mocha and Guatemala

Costa Rica, Sumatra and Hawaii

Java and Kivu or Tanzanian

Excelso from Columbia, Blue Mountain from Jamaica and
    Java

Many of these coffees may be enjoyed unblended, but their
qualities are not lost in blends and their contribution is well
noticed.

Colombian, Kenya and Costa Rica are particularly versatile
blenders. The milder-tasting coffees from the Americas are good
all-rounders with or without milk. The new crops are usually
acid. The stronger ones like Mocha, Mysore, Java and Sumatra
are best drunk black. Ethiopian Mocha may be used instead of
Mocha. Indonesian coffees are sometimes bitter; so are old
Bogotas and Brown Santos. Red Santos, Santo Domingo and
Haiti are sweet.

A mixture of light and dark roasted coffee is very pleasant. Try
three-quarters light and one-quarter dark, as the dark tends to
dominate, unless you are blending for Turkish coffee or espresso,
in which case it is nicer to have more of the darker one.

Coffee Classified–Market Terms

The wide variety of conditions, the mountains and the valleys,
the jungles and the plantations together with different species of
plants and more or less efficient pickers, combined with national
styles in marketing, have resulted in a great tangle of nomen-
clature. About forty producing countries use different systems of
classification for more than a hundred types of coffee.

Coffees are divided into three general groups.

Brazils include all coffees grown in Brazil. Apart from Santos,
they are of the cheaper types known as 'price' coffees, which make up

the bulk of mass-produced blends, most high roasts and those used for instant coffee.

Milds include all the *arabica* species grown elsewhere. These are the 'quality' growths. They are not necessarily mild to taste. Some are bitter or acidy.

Robustas are mainly grown in Africa from the different species of plant with that name. They are of inferior quality. Their high yield makes them formidable competitors on the 'price' coffee market.

There are four main important classes of taste.

Sweet is due to the sugar content which caramelizes on roasting and gives a liquorice colour to the brew.

Acidy is slightly sourish and sharp; is derived from the complex of compounds misnamed 'caffetanic acid'. Some beans, such as a new crop Santos, lose their acidity with age.

Bitter is due to decomposition products formed during roasting, as well as chlorogenic acid and the soluble mineral content of the bean when there is overextraction in the brewing process. Some beans also possess a certain natural bitterness.

Neutral is especially attractive for its versatility in everyday use and its blending qualities.

Coffees are further classified by:

Market names, usually those of the port of embarkation, or those of plantations or the area of production.

Species of plant, *arabica* being the quality growths.

Methods of processing: the 'washed' method is used for the choice beans.

Altitude, the high grown being always the finest.

By the number of imperfections, such as blackened, broken and immature beans, sticks, stones and pods.

According to size, shape and colour of beans: whether large or flat, and through all the shades of light green, grey and bluish-green. 'Hard-bean' indicates coffees of excellent body and acidity.

By the crop: whether old or new and the age of the trees.

By the age of the beans: most coffees improve with ageing between

5 and 10 years. Old Java especially matures exquisitely. Others, such as Bourbon Santos, weaken to a fragile insipidity.

By their drinking qualities.

This information may not help you to choose a coffee, but it will make you realize the complexity of the trade.

A Guide to the Choice Quality Beans

From the continents of Africa, India and the Americas as well as the islands that lie within the tropics I have chosen to list those coffees more worthy of note for their quality, and with a reputation that demands respect. I have also restricted the list to those more likely to be found in Britain, Europe and America. With the greater government control of more recent years, associations and co-operative selling, some of the famous historic names of coffee plantations have been absorbed into the different countries' productions. However, estates can still be recognized by perceptive buyers.

All the coffees listed are Milds, apart from Santos, the 'quality' Brazil. All mentioned are of the *arabica* variety. They are 'washed' and mostly high grown. The list is in alphabetical order.

ANGOLA

The world's fourth largest exporter produces only a very small amount of *arabica*, which is very similar to Brazilian Santos and as excellent in blends. Political upheavals have resulted in an uncertain production.

BRAZIL

A Portuguese Captain-Lieutenant of the Coastguard, Francisco de Malo Palheta, paying a visit to the Governor of Cayenne, French Guiana, in 1727, was so pleased with the coffee served to him that by ingratiating himself with the governor's lady, he managed to obtain secretly seeds of the coffee plant. With these he returned to the Portuguese Colony of Para on the Amazon river. Today, many types and grades make up 30 per cent of the world's total consumption.

Santos, especially Bourbon Santos (named after the French island colony of Bourbon, now Réunion, where the seed was grown), are the most popular for their sweet, clear, neutral flavour. They can be drunk straight but are also excellent partnered with any Mild. The true Bourbon is obtained from only the first few crops, which are grown from Mocha seed. After the third and fourth year, the bean changes in character. By the sixth it has become a Flat Bean Santos. Red Santos is sweet, Bourbon Santos is bitter, New Crop Santos is acidy. Ageing decreases the acidity.

The rest (Rio, Parana, Victoria, Bahia) are the less labour-intensive, mass-produced 'price' coffees; heavy, pungent and harsh, muddy and often peculiarly smoky from being dried on wood fires. They do, however, age well, losing their grassy flavour. Occasionally, accidents of nature such as the development of certain bacteria result in a special quality.

Although coffee will grow almost everywhere in Brazil, it suffers more than in any other country from unseasonable rains and storms, and winter winds which bounce out of the Andes. It is also permanently endangered by crippling frosts which dramatically lose a great deal of its production at least once every five years— on occasion as much as 80 per cent.

The chief plantations are on plateaux 1,800 feet to 4,000 feet above sea level. The two most fertile soils are 'terra roxa', a top soil of red clay three feet thick with gravelly subsoil in Sao Paolo and 'Massape', a yellowish soil.

Apart from the better grades, coffee is essentially a 'quantity' and not a 'quality' product. The planter's eye is on economy. In the giant *Fazendas*, care is not exercised in either cultivation or harvesting. Trees are not shaded, so the yield is greater, but the ripening is even more uneven. For quick picking whole branches are ripped off with unripe and over-matured beans, and to these are added those already fermented that have fallen on the ground.

BURUNDI

This country produces mainly *arabica*. The higher grades are rich with a good body and high acidity.

CAMEROON

Although cultivation is mainly of *robustas*, there are some fine, sweet, mellow *arabicas*. The round 'peaberries' (see 'Kenya') and giant 'elephant' beans are sorted out.

COLOMBIA

Colombia is the world's second largest producer after Brazil. There are many grades, from poor to first class. Some, among the world's best, have a beautiful flavour and aroma. Most popular are: Medellins (good acid flavour, mild taste, strong body, fragrant aroma); Excelso (has a slightly nutty bitterness); Manizales (more acidy); as well as Armenias, Libanos, Bogotas and Bucaramangas. Colombians produce a quarter more liquor of given strength than Brazilian Santos.

The finest grades are grown in the foothills of the Andes, 3,500 to 4,500 feet above sea level, in the shade of banana and rubber trees. Hundreds of thousands of small farms are family enterprises, organized into a federation on a co-operative basis. Great care is taken in cultivation and processing. Some of the best coffee lands consist of rich loamy soil mixed with disintegrated volcanic rock on porous subsoils.

COSTA RICA

The high altitude Costa Ricans are among the world's finest: rich in body, of fine mild flavour, sharply acid and fragrant. Some high grown varieties are said to be acidy enough to sour cream if used straight. The lower regions produce coffee of more neutral tastes. The most famous zone is the Central Plateau around San José, where the soil is rich black loam made up of continuous layers of volcanic ashes and dust three to fifteen feet deep. Beans are especially known for their fine preparation and screening.

The first plants were brought from Cuba in 1779 by a Spanish traveller, Navarro. Later, growths from Jamaica came with Padre Carazo, a Spanish missionary.

CUBA

Cubans are sold largely to Russia and Iron Curtain countries, but have recently appeared on the London market as a replacement to Jamaican coffees, to which they are similar in character.

DOMINICA

Somewhat sweet, the best grades are strong and heavy bodied with a peculiar, distinctive flavour. Dominicans are especially popular in the U.S.A. and West Germany.

ECUADOR

Ecuadors appear usually only in blends, as the taste is rather sharp and woody.

ETHIOPIA

The wild trees are the progenitors of all *arabicas* grown in the world. Carefully cultivated and high grown, Longberry Harar resembles Mocha, often replaces it and is also called Ethiopian

Mocha. It is highly acid with a winy flavour, good body, mild, gamy taste, very high yield and delightful aroma. Ethiopian (Abyssinian), more neutral in taste, is inferior and contains many imperfections. In the south-west there are vast areas of wild *arabica* trees practically untouched, where beans are just picked from the ground. These are the Djimma, Sidamo and Kaffa regions.

More recently attention has been given to improved methods of harvesting and preparation, and the industry has expanded. However, the produce of wild trees is still cleaned by wooden mortar and other primitive methods.

Some people believe that coffee derives its name from the region of Kaffa of which it is native. All the early legends about the discovery of the drink are based in Ethiopia. Though not much esteemed as a drink at first, it was consumed as a food. The beans were roasted, pulverized and mixed with butter to form hard balls to be eaten by the wandering Gallas on their journeys. Coffee was, however, an important export sent via Mocha—hence the early misconception of its origin.

GUATEMALA

Guatemalas are mild and mellow. The high grown have a fine acidity, heavy body and wonderful bouquet. Best known are Cobans and Antiguas. Some Cobans border on bitterness because of the extreme acidity.

On the lower highlands the trees are shaded by banana trees. On higher levels they are protected from cold north winds by hills. In severe weather rubbish and pitch is burnt to the north of the plantations. The dense smoke saves the trees from frost. Modern plantation machinery was introduced by German and American settlers.

HAITI

The best grades are sweet, mellow, rich in flavour, fairly acid and heavy bodied, resembling Jamaicans. The more carelessly cultivated grades of not too high quality are used for high roasts in Europe, where they are much appreciated.

Soil, climate and moisture are very favourable. Trees have always been allowed to grow wild. The political situation and the general lack of enterprise have resulted in a low production. Cultivation started here in 1715, and is the oldest in the western hemisphere.

JAMAICA

The high grown Jamaicans are the best of the West Indians. Blue Mountain is aristocratic and highly prized for its combination of all the attributes of a perfect coffee in quality, flavour, point and fullness. Hardly any has been available in England for four years. The Japanese, having recently adopted coffee, have been buying a great part of Jamaica's production. The low grown 'naturals' go into French roasts. The main coffee producing parishes are state owned.

Introduced in 1730, cultivation was encouraged and fostered by the British. Disastrous floods in 1815 and gradual exhaustion of the best lands led to the decline of the industry.

JAVA

These coffees are sometimes called Old Java, after the Old Government Java Coffees which had become a household word with their guaranteed minimum of ten years' tropical storage. Old Java also acquired an early reputation when, in the years before 1915, the natural sweating of the beans during their long voyage in slow-moving vessels on their way to New York resulted in a much-prized, uniquely musty flavour and a rare shade of brown.

Today, the best come from the Preanger, Cheribon, Buitenzorg and Batavia districts. They have a mature, subtle mellow flavour and impalpable spicy fragrance, good body and strength. They age extremely well, though they are not always allowed to do so.

Java is the oldest coffee producing country in which the tree is not indigenous. The plant was first introduced from Malabar at the instigation of the burgomaster of Amsterdam in 1699.

Other coffees from the Indonesian Archipelago, from Celebes (Sulawesi), Bali, Flores and Timor are often sold as Javas. They are equally good but crops are small and beans are hard to come by.

The *arabica* species has practically been driven out of the districts below 3,500 feet in altitude by leaf disease and has been succeeded by the more hardy *robustas* and *libericas* and their hybrids.

KENYA

One of the most delightful coffees, Kenya is extremely popular in Britain for its excellent flavour and fine acidity. In the much-prized Kenya Peaberry, one of the ovules never develops; the single ovule, having no pressure on one side, is round. It absorbs all the goodness of the cherry, which accounts for its fine quality and special liquoring.

Although it is indigenous to the African continent, coffee came from the island of Réunion with Roman Catholic missionaries as late as 1893. East African coffees entered the commercial market after the First World War and became popular in the United Kingdom after the Second World War. They have largely replaced coffees from India and Costa Rica on the London market.

KONA (from Hawaii)

This variety is named after the Kona district of Hawaii. Growths from Hawaii are all high grade and of superior quality with an excellent mild, smooth flavour and slight acidity. The most distinctive and deliciously rich coffee, full-bodied with a fine aroma and pungent exotic taste, grows on the dark volcanic lava in the Kona district, nestled between the twin towering volcanoes Mauna Loa and Mauna Kea.

Unfortunately, production is on the decline. Farmers are getting old, workers find alternative, more remunerative work in hotels. Younger growers are changing to Macadamia nut trees, which offer a much higher margin of profit. The industry might be a vanishing one.

MEXICO

Plants are said to have been transplanted here from the West Indies at the end of the eighteenth century by a Spaniard. Mellow, rich in body and of fine acidity, Mexicans have slight bitterness and pleasing bouquet. Best known are Coatepec, Huatusco and Orizaba. Coatepec rank with the world's best. The 'high grown' are cultivated on the Puebla Mountains. The 'prime washed' are grown in humid mountainous jungle-like regions and in low plantations.

MOCHA (from Yemen)

This is named after the Yemen city of Moka from which it was first exported, and which supplied all of the world's coffee trade until the close of the seventeenth century.

The dry Arabian soil and the lack of moisture in the air produce a bean which is extra-hard and small. Mocha has been recognized since the beginning of coffee drinking as the best available, with a clear, distinctive, winy, deliciously piquant, gamy flavour, a unique acid character that some consider aggressive and a very heavy body. It is valued as after dinner coffee, for a time of day when delicate flavours would go unnoticed. It blends well with most Milds, especially with Mysore and Indonesian growths (Java and Sumatra), and is a favourite for Turkish coffee blends often partnered with Mysore.

The crude and primitive cultivation has seen little improvement over the centuries. Trees are mostly grown in small gardens carved into the steep hillside of almost inaccessible mountain regions. An ingenious system of irrigation fed by mountain springs carries water to trees terraced with soil and small walls. All the work is done by hand. Beans are dried in the sun on housetops or on beaten earth.

Curiously, the drink is little appreciated and badly treated in the area where coffee was first cultivated. A weak decoction is generally made of the hulls. Small farmers are sadly neglecting coffee trees in favour of the drug 'qat' which is much in vogue for chewing. Production has also remained restricted because of political disturbances and uneconomical cultivation.

MYSORE (from India)

Other Indian coffees such as Coorg, Nilgiri and Malabar are often sold under the name of Mysore, the most celebrated of the Indians. It is also called Baba Budan after the Muslim pilgrim who brought back seeds from his Mecca pilgrimage in 1600 and planted them near his hut in the mountains of Mysore. The first systematic plantation was established in 1840 by the English in southern India.

Indian coffees have a distinctive velvety-soft, acid flavour, deep colour, heavy, strong body and delicate aroma. 'Monsooned' coffee has acquired a special flavour and a golden colour with the action of the south-west monsoon. The hot air has been allowed to circulate around loosely-stacked unwashed beans for about a month and a half. It is bought mainly by Norway, France and Sweden.

NICARAGUA

Nicaraguans are used mainly in blends, as they are not very distinguished.

PAPUA NEW GUINEA

The high grown Milds are grown from Kenya seeds and are of fine quality, resembling Kenya in type with a full, smooth flavour. This country is the most recent producer of all. Coffee was first grown commercially in the early 1950s and sold mainly to Australia and the U.S.A. It has only recently appeared on the English market, where its popularity is growing fast.

PERU

Peru coffees are full-bodied, delicate and gently acid. The best are grown at high altitudes on the slopes of the Andes. We might see more of Peru coffees on the English market, as the production is fast increasing.

PUERTO RICO

Puerto Rican coffee is delicious, sweet, richly flavoured and of high quality. Unfortunately, the dwindling production does not allow for exports to Europe, except for an annual offering to the Vatican.

RWANDA

The cultivation here is mainly of *arabicas*. The finest grow near Lake Kivu. They have good body, high acidity and a rich flavour.

SALVADOR

Neutral and mild in flavour, Salvadors are similar but slightly inferior in quality to Guatemalas. They are especially popular in Switzerland and Germany.

SUMATRA

The high grades are among the finest the world produces. Mandheling is perhaps the best, with a smooth, heavy body and almost syrupy richness of exquisite flavour and aroma. Ankola has a heavy body and rich, musky flavour. Ayer Bangies is very delicate in flavour. All are excellent for drinking black after dinner.

The climate and soil are ideal. Practically all the *arabica* coffee grows on the west coast. The east coast has more recently gone in for heavy planting of *robusta*. The industry was begun and fostered by the Dutch government, using forced labour, in 1699, with plants from the Malabar coast of India. The trade has diminished since Brazil and Central America became dominant in the market.

TANZANIA

Tanzanian is a fine coffee similar to Kenya but producing a thinner liquor. Most exquisite is Kibo Chagga, cultivated by the Chagga tribe in forest clearings on the cool and misty upper slopes of Mount Kilimanjaro.

VENEZUELA

Venezuelans are of excellent quality and among the world's best: mild and mellow, tender and delicate, acidy and with a slight but magnetic aroma. Much prized are Meridas, the best of the Maracaibos, which have a peculiar delicate flavour, neither acid nor bitter. Caracas has a light body and distinctive, pleasant flavour, and is especially popular in France and Spain. Caracas Blue is much in demand.

Some of the finest grades are grown on the slopes and foothills of the Maritime Andes, on the rich, well-drained soil in the equable climate and protective forest shade of the Caribbean coast, as well as on the fertile lowlands and valleys near the coast. Plantations are isolated and lack co-operative spirit. Methods of cultivation are old-fashioned.

ZAÏRE

Some fine *arabicas* are grown in the districts of Kivu and Ituri. These are excellent coffees, rich and highly acid, which may be used to add sharpness to milder blends.

Buying and Storing Coffee

For those within easy reach of a specialist coffee shop, the best way to buy coffee is in the bean, freshly roasted. And the best thing to invest in is a home grinder.

Although in its green state coffee ages well and is only adversely affected by dampness and strong odours which it absorbs, once roasted it begins to lose its aroma (the volatile complex caffeol) and will have lost most of it in two weeks. As soon as it is ground it loses it even faster, within a week. So only buy a little at a time, and grind it at home as you require it. Otherwise buy it already ground in very small quantities. It is possible to buy by mail order from most specialists. In this case buy whole roasted beans.

As soon as you open the greaseproof or foil-lined packet, empty the beans or ground coffee into an airtight jar; ground coffee in particular will not only go stale quickly, but will also embrace any nearby smells.

Coffee is not oversensitive about temperature, and I have not found any advantage in storing it in the refrigerator. However, American friends feel that coffee does keep better in the refrigerator. They also keep roasted beans in their freezer, but not for much longer than a month, and grind them while still frozen for immediate use.

A perfectly good and economical way of buying coffee is in the branded vacuum packs. Although quality and variety have to some extent been sacrificed by the dictates of competitive mass production, there are different blends, roasts and a certain range of grinders to choose from. Vacuum sealing machines close the container, which contains no air, but a little carbon dioxide gas. Atmospheric oxygen causes coffee to turn rancid in time. The tin assures that the aroma is sealed in. Plastic bags are equally effective and contain smaller quantities than the tins. Beans are also sometimes sold in these. A disadvantage with these mass-produced coffees is that the grind, generally medium coarse, is not suitable for every type of brewing method and the choice is thus limited. Finer, 'drip grind' coffee is easier to come by in the U.S.A. than in Britain.

Coffee bags are the most recent development in the convenience trade in roasted and ground coffees. When coffee essence is added to cut the brewing time the result is less than pleasant.

Roasting Coffee

Ideally every household, restaurant and café should have its own roasting equipment since coffee is better made with freshly roasted beans. Green beans are roasted to develop aroma, flavour and body, a practice started in the thirteenth century. During the process, chemical changes take place: soluble oils are developed, caramel is formed, adding its distinctive taste and giving coffee its rich brown shades, and gases are liberated inside the bean. These are the components of caffeol, which gives the precious aroma.

In the seventeenth and eighteenth centuries in England, coffee was browned over charcoal fires, in ovens and on top of stoves, in earthenware tart dishes, old pudding pans and frying pans. In Germany, where Frederick the Great had banned the consumption of coffee by ordinary citizens, it was the aroma of home roasting that led his 'coffee smellers' to discover those who were breaking the law.

Today it is mainly the poor and those from the less developed countries who do their own roasting. Various devices exist for this, but I have only seen two in this country. One is a small rotating perforated drum. The other is a covered pan with a top handle which turns an oar pushing the beans over and around.

Anyone can attempt their own roasting at home in a heavy frying pan if they are prepared to learn the hard way, by practice. It is not easy to achieve an even roast, but when you do, you will be rewarded by a magnificent aroma and a fine cup of coffee.

Use an old heavy pan. Have an open window or use an extractor to carry away smoke and chaff. Use only one layer of green beans; otherwise they will not roast evenly.

The best results are obtained from a medium slow fire at the beginning, then a quick high heat for development at the end. The quicker the roast, the better the coffee. Shake the pan constantly, stir and turn over the beans with a spatula or a wooden spoon so that the heat reaches the beans evenly on all sides. With Peaberry beans, which are rounded and roll about nicely in the pan, it is easier to get a more uniform roast. Do not panic if the beans start to brown unevenly. Some always do to begin with. They will shrivel up, become a yellowish brown, then swell, darken, and occasionally 'pop' open. Test a bean for readiness by biting into it or cracking it between your fingers. It must be thoroughly roasted inside as well as outside. Watch the colour. The art is to stop just before the desired degree of roasting has been reached. It takes practice. It might be sensible to strive at first for a medium brown. Never let the beans darken more than chocolate brown and be careful that the coffee oils do not catch fire. Remove from the fire and cool quickly (on marble is a good way) to preserve the aroma by closing the pores of the beans. The brown nuggets, evenly coloured from inside to outside, are ready for grinding as soon as they have cooled.

Another way of roasting coffee is in the oven. Put the beans in a roasting tin in a very hot oven, 475 °F (gas 9) for twenty minutes, shaking them occasionally. This will be enough for a mild to medium roast. For a high roast, reduce to 400 °F (gas 6) and leave another twenty minutes.

You may like to throw in spices towards the end of roasting, as Ethiopians do. Use cloves (5 to 8 for 8 cups of coffee), a small piece of cinnamon, ginger and nutmeg and sometimes cardamom or fennel seeds. Grind them together with the beans.

Most of us prefer to save ourselves the trouble and the disappointment of unevenly roasted beans, and rely on the skilled roaster at the specialist coffee shop. He watches over his beans being tossed about in the revolving cylinder placed alluringly at the shop window. He varies the heat slightly according to whether the coffee is new or old and dry, and thrusts in his 'trier', shaped like a long spoon, to see if they are done.

Automatic coffee plant operations work on the same principles as the small-capacity machines. Here cold water is often used to 'head' the roast. It turns to steam and is not absorbed, but just slightly swells and brightens the beans.

Finishing or glazing is practised to a small extent in the trade. A method of moist friction polish is common, as well as coatings of sugar and egg to make coffee more attractive. In the French (or Belgian) sugar roast, sugar caramelizes with the heat and makes a shiny black bean. It is also supposed to preserve the roasted bean and retain the aroma and oils. In 'Italian roast' a little butter is added with sugar to the cylinder.

Although terms and degrees of roasting are interpreted differently, four types are generally recognized in England.

Light or pale roast allows the milder beans to give their full delicate flavour and aroma, is recommended for breakfast and is good with milk.

Medium roast, for beans of a stronger character, gives a stronger coffee.

Full roast is not quite as 'burnt' as 'continental'.

Double or high roast, aptly called *'continental'* and *'after-dinner'*, has a strong bitter kick and should be drunk black. Cheaper growths are used. Choice ones would be wasted since much of the original flavour and aroma is driven off.

Europe and the Levant, as well as the producing countries, favour dark roasts, with Italians usually roasting to the point of carbonization. Americans like a medium roast while the feeling in the trade in England is that the more coffee is roasted, the more it loses its original aroma. Customers here having lately acquired a taste for high roasts through holidays abroad, a compromise has developed in the form of the very pleasant 'full roast'.

Grinding Coffee

To this day in the Middle East, pounding in a mortar, preferably wooden and with a stone pestle, is the method used to pulverize coffee. There is a beautiful song which traditionally accompanies the professional pounders, its rhythm easing the monotony of the affair. Generally, though, a long, deep groan emitted by the pounder at every blow of the heavy pestle wielded in two hands is the sound that you hear.

Brillat-Savarin, experimenting with pure Mocha beans, took it upon himself to establish which method, grinding or pounding, was to be preferred. He tasted coffee made with equal quantities of the two, and also submitted them to eminent connoisseurs. The unanimous verdict was that the coffee with the pounded powder was clearly superior to that made from the ground beans. Anyone is at liberty to repeat the experiment. For me, an electric grinder has proved less tiring and equally effective, though I cannot achieve as fine a pulverized flour for my Turkish coffee as my coffee shop does.

I have come across an antique utensil used for grinding, boiling and drinking, which at one time was part of the equipment of Turkish army officers. Perhaps an enterprising company will be inspired to make this collapsible, convertible coffee kit. Roasted beans are kept in the top section of the slender brass affair, which unscrews easily. To make a cup of coffee, the beans are taken out. A few are put in the middle section. A steel crank is fitted on to do the grinding. The ground coffee falls into the lower part, which acts as a pot. Water is added and it is brought to the boil on a fire. The bottom part also serves as a cup when the grounds have settled. When the cup has been rinsed out and dried, the remaining beans can be replaced and the utensil put together.

Many grinders exist on the market today, ranging from the old-fashioned hand grinders, which are coming back into fashion, to the electric ones that cut rather than grind. Most are equally efficient.

As soon as the tiny cells of fibrous tissues which make up the coffee beans are laid open, the precious aromatic oils and gases are released. Since the body and flavour of coffee are ground out, not boiled out, the quicker it is brewed after grinding, the better.

FINENESS OF GRIND

In choosing a mill, make sure that it is possible to adjust the coarse-ness of the grind over a fairly wide range. Most electric ones have whirling blades like a blender, and the degree of fineness is determined by the length of time the blades are allowed to cut. A few models are real mills, like electrically driven versions of hand grinders, and on these, the fineness is set by turning a wheel or screw.

The degree of fineness you want depends on your method of brewing and the length of your brewing cycle. The finer the grind, the more the coffee is exposed to the water, the greater the yield and therefore the shorter the brewing cycle required.

A *powdered or pulverized* coffee as fine as flour is used for Turkish coffee, where murkiness is not considered a disadvantage. It gives the maximum yield but loses some of the aroma in grinding. It is too fine for any of the other ways of making coffee.

Very fine, like cornmeal, is used for the *drip* and *filtration* methods when paper filters are used. The fine ground yields well and slows down the flow of water. A pulverized one would clog the filter. Any murkiness is banished from the liquor by the filter. It is also used for the Italian *espresso*, though small *espresso* machines, such as the 'Moka Express', work better with a very slightly coarser grind. Like powdered coffee, a very fine grind is more economical because of its high yield.

Fine, like granulated sugar, is used for *drip pots* and the Italian *Napoletana* pot with small perforations in the filter. It is also used in the vacuum method.

Medium is for coffee made in *the jug* by steeping and for *boiling up* to ensure that only a clear liquor is strained into the cups. More is needed, as the oils are less accessible to the water and the yield is smaller but the aroma has equally been better preserved for the brew. This grind is also used for the *pumping percolator* where a thinner grind would pass through the holes of the filter, and where the water has as much as seven or eight minutes to extract the maximum body from the coffee. Because of the weak extraction it is the least economical grind.

Although more of the aroma is lost to the air while grinding more finely, as far as storage is concerned, deterioration is faster in the coarser grind because of the ventilation. The finer the grind, the closer the particles pack together, the less the air can circulate through the mass, the less then the oxidation and the less aroma carried off.

Additives and Substitutes

The usual reason for additives in coffee is economy. Though chicory and figs are the only two that have achieved popularity for their own sake, many others have been tried in the past.

When Frederick the Great of Prussia made coffee an expensive state monopoly in 1781, the poorer classes had either to steal or to fall back on substitutes. They tried barley, wheat, corn, chicory and dried figs, roasted and ground. In England after the Great Fire in 1666, strange substitutes appeared such as betony (the root of a plant belonging to the mint family) as well as bocket or saloop, a decoction of sassafras and sugar.

General Sherman, in his memoirs of his experiences in the American Civil War, lists substitutes for the drink which had become indispensable for the soldiers, including Indian corn, sweet potato and the seed of the okra plant.

All types of grains, as well as sugar and molasses, and even pieces of bread, roasted and ground, have served as substitutes. An incredible variety of nuts, cereals and vegetables have been used at one time or another, from acorns and beans to beetroots and carrots, juniper berries and rice. Dandelion root is still used today and can be found ready-ground or in soluble form in health food shops. The list defies imagination. Apart from the caramel produced in roasting, it is a mystery to me how these substitutes could have tasted anything remotely like coffee.

A story is told of Prince Bismarck who, when in France with the Prussian army, entered a country inn one day and asked the host if he had any chicory in the house. He had.

'Bring it all then! All you have!'

The man obeyed, and brought a full canister and a couple of small boxes, half filled with chicory.

'Are you sure this is all you have?' asked the chancellor.

'Yes, my Lord, every grain.'

'Then,' said Bismarck, 'leave this here and now go and make me a pot of coffee.'

Some people would still like to do this in France, where there is a special fondness for chicory. Italians, Dutch and Germans like it, too, though in a lesser way. In England it is associated with the restrictive period of the last war, though some still like its slightly bitter taste, which they have acquired in those years. It is used in the catering trade to make coffee go further by giving it more colour and body.

The use of chicory originated in Holland in 1770. Chicory, succory or *Cichorium intybus* is a perennial plant which grows to a height of about three feet and bears pretty little blue flowers. Its leaves make a lovely salad. The long tap root is cut into slices,

dried in a kiln then roasted and ground in the same way as coffee.
Use about 20 per cent chicory with your coffee if you wish to
make your own mixture.

Another addition which is rapidly becoming popular in this
country is dried figs. This combination is now mass-produced
and known as Viennese coffee.

Packets of coffee with added spices have lately made an appearance in Cypriot shops in London. These are more in the line of
flavourings than additions and an innovation that might be an
interesting one for the trade to pursue.

Instant Coffee

'Nescafé no es cafe' (Nescafé is not coffee) is a slogan for purists
in Mexico, where soluble coffee has become the trendy drink, a
curious phenomenon which has overtaken many of the countries
where people have a coffee tree in their back garden. Nevertheless,
instant coffee is usually made with real coffee and with coffee alone.

Soluble coffee, with its unvarying taste, quickness of preparation and no grounds, came into its own during the First World
War, when it was shipped in large quantities to the American
forces serving in Europe.

Here the poorer grades from Brazil find oblivion. It is for the
avid and ever-growing instant coffee market that the *robusta* species
of the coffee tree is grown intensively in Africa, unrestricted and
without pruning or tending. The harsher tasting, high yield
robustas of Uganda, the sharp ones from the Ivory Coast and Togo,
the caffeine-rich beans of Zaïre and the coarse ones from Ghana
and the Sierra Leone are used in the blends. So, too, are the milder
robustas from the Congo, the neutral ones from Angola which are

so good that they might even be drunk straight, and those from Rwanda, Burundi and Nigeria with a strong liquor but not much flavour. The Indonesian islands also provide *robusta* beans for the soluble trade, and the Malagasy Republic and India have more recently entered into their production.

Whether in the national brands or in the private label coffees, the manufacture of dry soluble extracts has in some cases reached a reasonable degree of acceptability, with a variety of tastes and degrees of roasting. No method has yet been able to capture the fine aroma nor the unique subtleties of flavour of freshly made coffee, but the best do give a fair approximation, and are preferable to poorly made or stale coffee.

The most successful method of extracting the drinking properties from ground roasted beans is by freeze-drying. It is generally the most expensive, and employs the better quality beans in the cheaper range. It only takes 6 per cent of the instant market. In this method coffee is brewed, the liquor is frozen into slabs and ground into particles (sizes of particles are usually chosen for their visual appeal). These are passed through a tunnel with a high vacuum and a very small amount of heat. The ice and water elements are removed from the frozen particles by sublimation. This turns the ice straight to steam, without turning into water, leaving the particles dry and chunky.

The most common and cheaper method which takes up all the rest of the market is by spray drying. The water from a concentrated (and unfortunately overextracted) liquid is evaporated, leaving only coffee powder or hollow spherical particles according to the design of the nozzle. Requiring high heat, this process changes the character of the soluble material and drives off the volatile constituents which make the natural flavour. 'Agglomerated' versions of these methods aim at a texture more akin to that of real coffee, but are no improvement on flavour. Spraying with coffee oil sometimes returns a little of the aromatics, but the effect is evanescent, and also brings the problem of rancidity.

Instant coffee is particularly attractive for flavouring cakes and puddings where no extra water is required. A liquid coffee essence, the most common type of coffee sold in this country until after the war, in the familiar slim square bottle, is also reasonably good for flavouring. Otherwise, as a coffee man pointed out, it is excellent for staining wood floors.

Instant coffee may be used in all the ways described in the section on serving coffee. One teaspoon in a coffee cup is the usual quantity required. Pour freshly boiled water over it and stir.

Brewing Coffee

In 1845 Eliza Acton wrote: 'There is no beverage which is held in more universal esteem than good coffee and none in this country at least which is obtained with greater difficulty. We hear constant and well founded complaints from foreigners and English people of the wretched compounds so commonly served up here under its name.'

Sadly, things have not much changed today. A coffee man, head of one of the most important firms of mass-produced coffees, confided to me that he usually started his lectures to Women's Institutes with the phrase 'Not one of you can make coffee properly!' followed by the questions 'Which one of you warms the pot? Which one waits the full four minutes for the coffee to brew?' He plays on the lack of confidence which spoils coffee-making for the great majority.

Curiously, the simple truths have so far kept themselves veiled in exotic mystique. There is nothing mysterious or difficult about making coffee. Yet so sensitive is it to improper handling that it will not live up to its aromatic and flavoursome promise unless it is made with love.

Various methods find advocates, for reasons of taste, culture, habit and lifestyle. Each method achieves a certain distinctive character. It is worth trying them all to discover your preference before becoming a victim of habit. Nor is there anything wrong in developing a taste for one particular style. Familiarity can develop the ritual of brewing to a fine art.

Although there are many types of equipment, none is essential to make an excellent coffee with fully developed flavour, aroma, strength and body. All you may need is a jug or a saucepan. However, there are some very efficient and attractive pots and devices about, each providing a brew that varies slightly from that of the others.

Coffee does not need to be cooked. The roaster has already 'cooked' it and developed the aromatic constituents sufficiently so that they are ready to be dissolved in hot water when the cells of the beans have been thoroughly opened by grinding. All that is required from brewing is to extract the already cooked aromatic constituents from the surrounding fibrous tissue. This may be perfectly well achieved by the short contact of boiling water with coffee.

Brewing is a matter of either boiling or infusion, and all the innumerable devices for making coffee, including steeping, filtration, pumping percolation, vacuum and pressure, work on these two basic principles.

With infusion, boiling water, which has cooled slightly as it is poured, extracts the caffeine and the aromatic constituents without driving away the aroma. Provided that overextraction does not occur through reheating or overheating or allowing the grounds to stand in the liquor for too long, the bitter and astringent components of roasted coffee will be left undissolved in the grounds. This method preserves the utmost aroma for the cup and obtains the maximum and purest flavour. It is therefore not surprising that infusion and in particular filtration is by far the most popularly acclaimed in the West.

Although to American pundits and epicures, making coffee in any other way is sacrilege and a perversion of taste, half the world still loves strong bitter coffee, boiled as in the Turkish and Arab ways or, as in the Italian espresso, overextracted by the action of steam. Even in America, 60 per cent of the coffee-drinking households persist in using the much criticized but ubiquitous pumping percolator which boils the liquor continuously for several minutes.

When coffee is boiled, there is a certain decomposition and some of the less soluble materials of an astringent and more bitter nature are dissolved, while much of the aroma (the caffeol) is steam-distilled from the brew. Many people, however, are addicted to coffee made in this way. Bitterness, an acquired taste, is also one of the basic natural tastes of coffee. When it is strong it gives an extra kick to the stimulating brew, one which perhaps makes up for the loss of some of the aroma. Admittedly, in many of the countries where coffee is boiled, the bitterness is usually mitigated by sugar and often by the perfume of spices, and of course only a little is drunk at a time, in very small cups.

Apart from the bitterness resulting from overextraction, which may be unpleasant for many people, there is the special tang obtained from the strong flavour of high roasted beans. There is also the more attractive bitterness of strong coffee, which is simply a concentration of the normal bitter taste, as in the French 'demitasse' and the Italian 'ristretto'. The strength of a brew depends, of course, on the amount of coffee used. The required amount is a matter of taste and is also related to the method of brewing and the fineness of grind, since the finer the grind and the longer the brewing cycle the greater the yield. Coffee might be too weak as a result of the grind being too coarse, the extraction time too short or the water not being hot enough. American experts have established that a perfect brew contains soluble solids at 19 per cent (of its own weight) of extraction. More than that results in bitterness. This perfect brew is easily obtained by following good brewing practices.

Now make your coffee. Having bought good quality, freshly roasted beans, grind them just before you use them, or use a ground vacuum-packed blend. Brew your coffee affectionately so that it yields the utmost of its delights. The best method is a matter of personal taste. For me, the type of coffee I enjoy most is a matter of mood, of time of day, and of place.

To make a perfect cup of coffee some general points are important. Cold, freshly drawn water must be used, the purer and the softer the better. Any salts or chemicals in it will spoil the taste.

The grind must be of the right fineness for the chosen method. The pot must be warmed.

When making an infusion, the water *must* come into contact with the ground coffee at *just under boiling point* (205 °F.) to extract the oils and aromatic principles from the cells.

Always make coffee at full strength, as there is nothing more insipid than a weak diluted drink. As a general rule, with a fine grind you will need one rounded tablespoon of ground coffee (about 0·35 oz. or one Approved Coffee Measure) to a coffee-cupful (about 7½ fl. oz.) of water. I like it extra strong and use a rounded tablespoon to 5 or 6 fl. oz. of water. If you want a double strength 'demitasse', use one rounded tablespoon to half the quantity of water (about 4 fl. oz.). If you are using a coarser grind, you may need as much as 4 rounded tablespoons to a pint of water. The quantity of coffee required varies a little according to the method, since the longer the water is allowed to act on the coffee, the less is needed. Also, the finer the grind, the greater the yield, the less coffee required. Ultimately, of course, personal taste dictates the strength or weakness of the perfect cup. For a weaker infusion, do not use less grounds with the usual amount of water, as this results in overextraction of the less pleasant, more bitter and woody elements of the bean. Make it regular strength, and dilute it. For the same reason do not use less of a high yielding (such as pulverized) grind with a longer brewing cycle.

Drink the coffee hot, as soon as it is made. An hour later it will have lost its aroma.

Reheat coffee if necessary *au bain marie*, in a saucepan of boiling water, and not by bringing it to the boil. Some people like to keep black coffee hot in a Thermos flask.

Keep coffee covered if you are going to drink it later.

Not all metals are suitable for brewing, as coffee liquor reacts chemically with some, affecting the taste of the coffee. Iron and aluminium should be avoided. Silver, tinned copper and enamelled iron may be used without any risk of contamination. Otherwise earthenware and glass make the best containers. Although aluminium is often used, it does give an odd aftertaste.

And, of course, never re-use coffee grounds; and do wash your equipment well, as grounds and oils soon become rancid.

TURKISH COFFEE

The 'black mud' sucked by the Levantines prevails throughout the Middle East up to Greece, North Africa and the Balkans. As the Frenchman, Thevenot, already wrote in the seventeenth century: 'One must drink it hot, but in several instalments, otherwise it is no good. One takes it in little swallows for fear of burning one's self—in such fashion that in a *cavekane* (café) one hears a pleasant little musical sucking sound.' He was talking of the Turkish version of Arab coffee which was originated in the early sixteenth century, adding sugar and just bringing it to the boil three times, instead of boiling for a long time.

William Lane so well describes coffee-making in Egypt in the mid-nineteenth century, when sweetened coffee had not yet become popular, that I would like to give his account from *The Manners and Customs of the Modern Egyptians*.

'The coffee (*kahweh*) is made very strong, and without sugar or milk. The coffee-cup (which is called *finggan*) is small, generally holding not quite an ounce and a half of liquid. It is of porcelain, or Dutch-ware, and, being without a handle, is placed within another cup (called *zarf*) of silver or brass, according to the circumstances of the owner, and, both in shape and size, nearly resembling an egg cup. In preparing the coffee, the water is first made to boil: the coffee (freshly roasted, and pounded) is then put in, and stirred; after which the pot is again placed on the fire, once or twice until the coffee begins to simmer; when it is taken off and its contents are poured out into the cups while the surface is yet creamy. The Egyptians are excessively fond of pure and strong coffee thus prepared; and very seldom add sugar to it and never milk or cream; but a little cardomom seed (*hababan*) is often added to it. It is a common custom, also, to fumigate the cup with the smoke of mastic and the wealthy sometimes impregnate the coffee with the delicious fragrance of ambergris. The most general mode of doing this is to put about a carat-weight of ambergris in a coffee pot, and melt it over a fire; then make the coffee in another pot in the manner before described and when it has settled a little, pour it into the pot which contains the ambergris. Some persons make use of the ambergris, for the same purpose in a different way; sticking a piece of it, of the weight of about two carats in the bottom of a cup and then pouring in the coffee; a piece of the weight above mentioned will serve for two or three weeks. This mode is often adopted by persons who like always to have the coffee which they themselves drink flavoured with the perfume, and do not give all their visitors the same luxury.'

The orientalist Richard Burton also describes the use of ambergris in coffee in *Love, War and Fancy*.

'The egesta of the whale, found in lumps weighing several pounds in the sea on the coast of Zanzibar, is sold at a high price being held a potent aphrodisiac. A small hollow is drilled in the bottom of the cup and the coffee is poured upon the bit of ambergris it contains; when the oleaginous matter shows in dots amidst the *kaymagh* (coffee cream), the bubbly froth which floats upon the surface, an expert "coffee servant" distributes it equally among the guests.'

I personally have not seen anyone flavouring with ambergris, whereas I have seen many using cardamom, cinnamon, nutmeg and cloves. Cardamom is particularly popular, dropped into the pot while it is boiling. Some people open the pod, extract one seed and use this alone in the coffee.

Method: Make it in an *ibrik* (or *kanaka*), a smallish long-handled metal pot made of tinned copper or brass. If one is not available, use a small saucepan. *Ibriks* come in various sizes. The number of coffees they will make is often scratched on the underside. If you do not know, measure the capacity with small coffee cups. Beans should be roasted medium high or continental and ground to a fine powder.

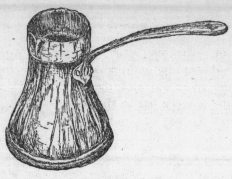

Ibrik

For two coffees:
2 very heaped teaspoons of pulverized coffee
2 very heaped teaspoons of sugar or to taste
2 small coffee cups of water

Boil the water with the sugar. Add the coffee, stir well and return
to the fire. When the coffee froths up to the rim, remove from the
fire. Repeat twice again. Some let a drop of cold water precipitate
the grounds; others rap the pot smartly; others still let them
settle by waiting.

You might like to add spices. Try one at a time. Put them in the
ibrik to boil with the water. Try a cardamom pod, a couple of
cloves, a small stick of cinnamon or a pinch of freshly grated
nutmeg.

Serve as soon as the grounds have settled while still hot. Pour
or rather shake out a little froth for each cup. Some grounds will
settle at the bottom of the cup. You are not supposed to eat them.
As Dufour said, 'In the Levant it is only the scum of the people
who swallow the grounds.' But you can make use of them. Some
people, usually women, profess to be able to read fortunes in the
trickle of the grounds in an upturned cup. Grounds also have
medicinal value, properties which have been borne out in scientific research; deodorant, antiseptic, germicidal and bactericidal.

I am tempted to relate a scatological anecdote which illustrates the double virtue of spent grounds.

'A man went to see his doctor complaining of haemorrhoids. The doctor advised him to drink coffee six or seven times a day and each time to go and wash the painful parts and rub them well with the grounds left at the bottom of the cup. After a week of applying the cure assiduously, the patient returned to his doctor who asked him to remove his trousers and to bend down. Taking a close look and after due reflection, the doctor said with trepidation: "I can see a tall young blonde coming into your life".'

BOILING UP IN A SAUCEPAN

Although to the Western coffee pundits and epicures 'boiling' is anathema to good coffee and the worst possible way of making it, the method continues to find advocates in every country, especially in rural areas where it dieshard.

Of course the West might have been put off by the early methods of boiling that prevailed. In England coffee was boiled for a long time. An egg white was dropped in during boiling to capture the finest particles of ground when it coagulated, dragging them down to the bottom. Sugar candy was not infrequently stirred into the drink, and so too were mustard, salt and pepper.

In the Far West of America coffee was simmered in a pot or saucepan for two or three hours, and could be kept for as long as a week and reheated as required. The coffee pot was never washed so as not to lose the collected aroma of a thousand makings. America's hardy drinkers liked their coffee 'hot, black and strong enough to walk by itself'. Many variations were in vogue, such as mixing the grounds with egg yolks, white and shell before boiling; another involved codfish for extra taste and colour. Both fish and egg techniques were still popular in the late nineteenth century.

Method: Put water and medium coarse grounds, one rounded tablespoon per coffee cupful (4 rounded tablespoons for 1 pint) into

a pot or covered saucepan. Only just bring to the boil, then leave
to rest 5–8 minutes to infuse further. A drop of cold water will
encourage the grounds to settle. Keep warm under a tea-cosy.
Pour through a fine strainer straight into cups or into a serving
pot which should be warmed by rinsing in hot water.

This is an excellent method of making coffee for a large party—it
does not foster a bitter taste as longer boiling would, nor does it
drive away the aroma, but the coffee is usually a little cloudy as a
result of the disintegration of grounds by even the slightest
violence of boiling. This may be removed by straining through a
cloth filter. Some shops sell a nylon 'sock' fixed to a plastic rim.

AN INFUSION

Various ways of making a simple infusion find the most favour
with coffee lovers all over the world. Steeping the grounds in
water just under boiling point, without further boiling, preserves
the utmost aroma and flavour without allowing a trace of bitterness. The drip, filter and jug methods work on the same principle.

The idea first appeared in France in 1711 for making coffee *sans
ébullition* (without boiling) in the form of a cloth bag containing
grounds dropped inside the coffee pot over which boiling water is
poured—a device still in use in many countries. Its main drawback
is that keeping the bag clean and hygienic requires a great deal of
attention. It must be washed and left in fresh water until it is
used again.

THE DRIP POT

In 1800, the Archbishop of Paris, Jean Baptiste de Belloy, devised
a pot which is still today the model for many a drip pot (called
'percolateur' in France). It was given the accolade by Brillat-
Savarin. Most pots are in three parts. The top receives the water,
a bottom pot receives the coffee and there is a coffee basket in
between the two.

Method: Preheat the pot by scalding with hot water. Measure the
necessary amount of medium ground coffee into the filter section

Two drip pots:

French Drip

Machinetta Napoletana

(perforated chinaware or metal). Pour the required amount of fresh boiling water into the upper container, then cover. When all the liquid has dripped through, remove the upper section and serve.

Many drip pots exist. Porcelain ones are the best and the most used, but there are also silver and aluminium ones. These have the disadvantage of allowing more heat loss, and aluminium leaves an aftertaste. However, unlike porcelain ones they can be kept warm on a hotplate while the coffee drips. *Café filtre*, individual drips placed over a cup in French cafés, are often slow to run through and need some encouragement by applying pressure with the palm of the hand if they are to fill the cup before the coffee is cold. With the *Napoletana*—the Neapolitan two-tiered *machinetta*, water is boiled in the bottom part of a coffee pot which is then turned over to allow the boiling water to run slowly through a central filter containing the grounds. The top part, furnished with a spout, becomes the bottom part, ready for pouring.

THE FILTER

In this most popular and most satisfactory form of the drip method, a cone-shaped paper filter bag removes all traces of the slightest sediment, resulting in a perfectly clear, flavoursome liquor. A fine grind which gives a maximum yield should be used. Pulverized coffee would clog the filter and stop the flow of liquor, and a coarse grind would let the water run through too quickly and make for a weak brew. Individual filters are available for single cups. Larger ones fit over jugs. Coffee correctly brewed in this way is unfailingly clear, fragrant and seductive—but the device must be properly handled. The most successful of the automatic coffee-makers use this method.

Method: Preheat the pot by scalding. Insert filter bag into dry filter. Measure fine ground coffee into filter (one measuring spoon, usually provided with the device, per cup). Moisten coffee with boiling water to cover and gently shake the filter so that no dry lumps remain. Allow to steep for half a minute, then top up filter

Melitta

to the required level. You can keep the heatproof jug warm during the filtering on a very low flame or a hotplate.

IN A JUG

So like brewing tea, this manner is obviously the most popular in England and is the one recommended by most people in the coffee trade today. It is inexpensive, as they point out, since no equipment is required, only a pot or jug, and a strainer. In her book *The Rosary*, Florence L. Barclay has a Scotswoman tell how she makes coffee. She says:

'Use a jug—it is not what you make it in; it is how ye make it. It all hangs upon the word fresh—freshly roasted—freshly ground—water freshly boiled. And never touch it with metal. Pop it in an earthenware jug, pour in your boiling water straight upon it, stir it with a wooden spoon, set it on the hob ten minutes to settle; the grounds will go to the bottom, though

you might not think it, and you pour it out, fragrant, strong
and clear. But the secret is fresh, fresh, fresh and don't stint
your coffee.'

Instructions are still the same today.

Melior

Method: Warm the pot by scalding. Measure the required amount
of medium-ground coffee (too fine results in a cloudy liquor) into
the pot. Use at least four heaped tablespoons for one pint of water.
Pour on freshly boiling water and stir thoroughly with a wooden
spoon. Keeping the pot warm under a tea-cosy or on a hotplate,
allow the coffee to stand for four to six minutes to brew and
settle. Skim the froth from the top. Pour through a strainer,
taking care not to disturb the grounds which have settled at the
bottom of the jug.

Use more than four tablespoons if you like a strong brew, since
the medium-grind does not yield as much as a fine one. A simple
version, used in a few countries, is to pour boiling water on

grounds straight into the cup. Modern coffee-makers which work on the same principle, such as the Melior, have recently appeared on the market. A plunger unit attached to the lid acts as an inside strainer. In fine glass, with a silver or gold frame, they are very attractive to bring to the table.

THE PUMPING PERCOLATOR

A device that made its appearance in 1825 and enjoyed a certain vogue through the nineteenth century is the one that finds the least favour today. A weak infusion liquor is boiled and recirculated by the pumping action of steam until a satisfactory degree of extraction has been reached. The continuous boiling produces a certain bitterness. The main advantage is that it requires less coffee, since the water acts on it for a longer time. Although it is still used in the majority of American coffee-drinking homes, this method has become the target for the anger of the trade, who blame it for the declining sales of the last decade.

Method: Pour the required amount of fresh cold water into the percolator. When the water boils, remove from the heat. Measure the

Pumping Percolator

required amount of medium-ground coffee into the basket and insert the basket into the percolator. Cover, return to heat and allow to percolate gently for 6 to 8 minutes. Remove the basket with the grounds and serve.

THE VACUUM OR GLASS BALLOON

An international favourite, this makes an excellent coffee in an extremely attractive way. The glass container exhibiting the warm colours of coffee developing adds to the pleasantly sensuous ritual of making coffee at the table. Its reputation has, unfortunately, been somewhat tarnished by the many restaurants and hotels that use the device to make coffee in advance and warm it up before serving. Robert Napier, a Scottish marine engineer, invented the first model in 1840, an extraordinary device with a magical-looking silver globe, a syphon, a strainer and a mixing bowl.

Method: Pour the necessary amount of fresh cold water into the lower bowl and place on heat. Place filter into upper funnel and add the measured quantity of medium fine or fine coffee. Place over the lower bowl and twist to seal tightly. Place on heat and bring to the boil. When the water has risen into the funnel, stir coffee and water well. When it has ceased to rise, leave on the heat a further minute, then turn off. When all the coffee has filtered down into the lower bowl, remove the funnel and serve.

THE ITALIAN ESPRESSO

The espresso coffee machine, invented by the Italian Achille Gaggia, in 1946, became the success story of the fifties in Britain. It was responsible for the rash of coffee bars which started in Soho and spread throughout the country. The Moka Bar was the first to open in Frith Street. The Coffee Inn in Park Lane, Mocambo in Knightsbridge and the Boulevard in Wigmore Street, all became instantly popular. Young people could meet casually at the Gondola, El Cubano or Kardomah over a cup of coffee in a contemporary décor, which then meant tiles, wickerwork, bare

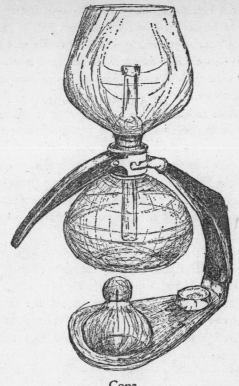

Cona

bricks and matting. The style was exotic with tropical vegetation, homely and rustic with bunches of onions and garlic, or Italian with fleets of gondolas and Chianti bottles holding candles—a real departure from the old snack-bars of England. Pottery-makers and glass-blowers twisted their wares into fantastic shapes for the dark subterranean bars and the brilliantly lit houses of fantasy. The sound of a parrot or of a Spanish guitar carried the drinkers away into strange, far-off places. Social needs were met, but the standard of the brew was well below the one produced by the same machines in Italy. Even with an Italian behind the machine, the coffee served was invariably poor.

Well-made espresso is one of the best-loved coffees in the world. Home-brewing Moka-type pots work on the same steam pressure principle as the big machines. On account of the pressure, the water boils at a higher temperature than normal. Steam is forced through the grounds, extracting more from them than boiling water normally does. Unfortunately, in England it is not possible to find large enough Moka-type pots to make more than about six cups of ordinary size.

A high roast is recommended for this type of coffee, which is rather strong if the measures on the pot are followed. A slight bitterness results from the extraction under pressure. The following method is for a Moka-type pot, of which the original brand is called the 'Moka Express'. There are now many rivals; the newest types, at present available only in Italy, are made of stainless steel and avoid the problems of the original aluminium ones.

Method: Separate the top and base by unscrewing. Remove the filter funnel and fill the base with enough water to reach the safety valve. Fill the filter funnel with finely ground coffee without pressing the coffee down. Replace the funnel and screw the top firmly to the base. Place over heat. As soon as coffee begins to rise to the top through the stem, lower the heat to a minimum. A

Moka Express

bubbling noise indicates that all the water in the lower part has risen through the grounds. Remove from heat; when coffee stops rising it is ready to serve.

The rubber washer needs replacing occasionally and remember not to leave the pot over heat when there is no water left in the base. If you leave the pot unused for more than a few days, scrub it with hot water and a stiff brush just before you use it again.

Serving Coffee

For the purist, the only way to drink coffee is black, or *nature* as the French call it. Across the Channel that usually means very strong, from a high roast, sometimes burnt almost to a char, and served *en demitasse*, the traditional small after-dinner cup.

For *café nature* use one heaped tablespoon of ground coffee to to each ¾ cup (4 fl. oz.) of water. The higher yield of the Italian espresso method results in the extra strong *ristretto*. *Lungo* is their weaker version, served in larger cups.

Serve it very hot (about 75 °C.) as soon as it is made. There is little pleasure in lukewarm coffee, and an hour later it will have lost its precious aroma. If the liquor has not been filtered, pour it gently without disturbing the grounds, as though decanting ancient wine. Drink it sensitively like wine, appreciating the bouquet and the colour. It is not affectation but simply making the most of what is good.

Coffee has made some highly successful marriages of flavour, some no doubt by happy chance, which are well worth trying out. A pleasant sensation for the palate is the use of lemon in coffee.

In Italy and many other parts of the world, a strip of lemon peel is often curled round the rim of the cup. Add excitement to your drink with a sprinkling of grated lemon or orange peel, or, as in the old Russian way, with a squeeze of lemon juice.

Moroccans like to use whole black peppercorns to give extra kick. They may add a pinch of salt, a habit also popular in Ethiopia, to bring out the finer flavours. As Simone Beck points out, 'The flavour of even the finest coffee will be enhanced if at the moment of pouring boiling water over the coffee, one adds a tiny pinch of salt.' Lately in the Americas, people have become fond of flavouring with honey, a very pleasant alternative to sugar. Spices, introduced in the Levant, and used extremely lightly, will add a fugitive impression. Try stirring the brew with a stick of cinnamon as they do in Italy, or sprinkle with a pinch of powder.

I have lately been served an Arab coffee by Saudi Arabians from a stocky, birdlike brass coffee-pot. Pulverized coffee had been boiled with water as in Turkish coffee. The unsweetened brew was filtered into an identical pot through a piece of *loufa* squeezed into the spout. Here, freshly pounded saffron pistils and carda-mom seeds gave it a delicate and most intriguing perfume.

My friend Elizabeth Lambert Ortiz gives a recipe for a Mexican *Café de olla* in her *Mexican Cooking*. It is traditionally made and served in earthenware bowls, but she suggests using a saucepan for making a larger quantity.

Heat four cups of water with half a cup of *piloncillo* (Mexican or other brown sugar), a two-inch stick of cinnamon, and four cloves in a saucepan or a heatproof coffee-pot, stirring until the sugar is dissolved. Add four tablespoons of dark roasted ground coffee, bring to the boil and simmer for a minute or two. Stir, cover and leave on the stove in a warm place for the grounds to settle. Serves four.

Strong black coffee, even high-roasted, is delightful served with fresh cool cream, whether whipped and floating lightly or thick and run slowly down the back of a spoon so that its weight does not pull it straight to the bottom.

❧LACED COFFEE❧

An excellent after-dinner habit is to take coffee laced with a spirit or a liqueur. The French *cordial* or the Italian *corretto*, equally good at other times of the day, is said even by the puritanical to aid digestion. Others simply love it.

You need not use the élite of spirits, those which bear their place of origin like a coat of arms. An *eau de vie* from the local cottage industry, distilled from any fruit, is likely to be as good.

In grapeless Normandy, the least refined kind of Calvados, a distilled cider from local apples, is poured into a half-full cup of coffee to fill it to the brim. In the South of France, Marc, a spirit made from grape skins and pips, is drunk with coffee, also in equal quantities. Poire is a Belgian favourite, and in Switzerland, Kirsch made of cherry stones. Other *alcools blancs* made of apricots, blue plums, raspberries and strawberries are excellent. Cognac, of course, is extravagant but its special raciness and excitement is inimitable; and the more rustic Armagnac has an equally spirity and fiery quality.

We on this side of the Channel know the special delight of coffee with gently sweet and smoky whisky. Whether you use Scotch, Irish or Bourbon, use a blended variety, whose anonymity will not suffer from mixing with an alien brew. Crème de menthe and Anis (or Ouzo or Arak) give a fine freshness to coffee. You must also try the sweet luxury of Cointreau and Bénédictine, of Curaçao and Crème de Cacao, as well as the excitement of vodka and the sharpness of Strega. Rum is magnificent in coffee. The pungent, fiery distilled essence of sugar cane brings the fruity-spice flavour of the Caribbean to a memorable cup. And, of course, Tia Maria, the coffee liqueur, is a natural companion.

Use the less delicate and more savage of these great spirits and liqueurs, but if you only have the superior products it is not a sacrilege to slip a little in the cup. It will not be wasted.

Fill a small cup only three-quarters full of strong hot black coffee. Sweeten it if you like and add a jigger or a dash of a favourite spirit.

With Cognac brandy, coffee is not surprisingly called 'Café Royal'. Put a cube of sugar in a tablespoon. Pour brandy over it to fill the spoon. Set it alight and quickly pour it into the coffee. Coffee and brandy in equal parts, flavoured with vanilla, is called 'Café Gloria'.

The fondness for alcohol in coffee is not confined to Europe. Laced coffees are also very popular in the Americas. Here, cream, thick and heavy or whipped and light, is an added delight to the rum and to the numerous fruit and other liqueurs of South America. The mixture comes garnished with a strip of lemon peel and topped with cream. Cream is also used in one of the most famous drinks of all, Irish coffee. I must go into more detail with this, since it is part of our heritage.

IRISH COFFEE

Into a warmed, large wineglass put two jiggers of Irish whiskey and one teaspoon or more of sugar to taste. Pour in freshly made hot coffee and stir. As the contents revolve, add a jigger of double cream, dribbling it slowly over the back of a spoon into the drink. Allow the cream to float to the top and do not stir.

CAFE AU LAIT

Inspired by the drinking of tea with milk, Nieuhoff, the Dutch Ambassador to China, was officially the first person to try coffee with milk, around 1660.

The French breakfast drink is traditionally served in large bowls on which you can warm your hands, or in cups large enough to dip a piece of *baguette*, a *croissant* or a *brioche*. Hot milk and extra-strong coffee are poured from two pots simultaneously into the cup. Proportions vary from half-and-half to one part milk and three parts coffee. It is for you to decide how you like it.

In Vienna, whose coffee has been described as without equal, two parts of coffee to one of hot milk is called *melange* and topped with whipped cream. *Brauner* coffee is darker and *schwarzer* is without milk. In Italy equal parts of hot milk and strong coffee make *caffè latte*, while *capuccino* is sprayed with hot, frothy milk forced from a syphon, or better still, with whipped cream, and is powdered with cinnamon or nutmeg or a little grated orange peel.

A delicious alternative to 'café au lait' relies on the special affinity of the sister berries, chocolate and coffee. The alliance usually termed Mocha, after coffee's first port of export, is variously interpreted and exotically named Café Borgia, Viennese Coffee, Javanese hot Mocha and Mexican Negrita.

CAFÉ BORGIA OR VIENNESE COFFEE

This can be made with plain chocolate (sweet, unsweetened or semi-sweet), powdered drinking chocolate or cocoa powder. Ordinary block chocolate is perhaps the best.

To make four delicious cups, gently melt four ounces of chocolate in a saucepan, being careful not to burn it. Add sugar or honey to taste and stir in four tablespoons of cream. Pour in four cupfuls of hot, freshly made coffee a little at a time, beating well till frothy. Keep hot over a small fire. Serve with whipped cream and sprinkle with a little ground cinnamon, cocoa or grated orange peel. A spiced version uses four cloves and a stick of cinnamon brewed with the coffee and strained or filtered with the grounds. If you are making one cup only, it may be easier to use drinking powdered chocolate. Some, such as Brazilians, like to pour hot milk on the chocolate and add it to an equal quantity of strong hot coffee. A Javanese Mocha is sometimes topped with marshmallow cream.

Whatever it is called, I suspect the marriage of coffee and chocolate originates in Mexico, where the Spanish Conquistadores first found Montezeuma's courtiers drinking cups of chocolate. For their 'Negrita', Mexicans brew coffee with the usual spices, beat it with an equal quantity of strong cocoa and serve it with whipped cream.

HAWAIIAN COFFEE

This delightful drink, popular in the Caribbean, is made with coconut.

Heat an equal quantity of milk and grated coconut in a saucepan over a low fire until it is creamy. Strain, and put the coconut under a grill to brown. Add the hot 'coconut milk' to an equal quantity of double strength, freshly made hot coffee. Sweeten to taste and serve sprinkled with the browned coconut.

COFFEE PUNCHES

Festive versions of cordials providing the palate with a variety of exotic perfumes, these punches can be made in a saucepan, but a chafing dish or a silver bowl at the table and elusive flames in the darkness provide a fitting sense of drama.

The quantities I give will serve about eight to ten people.

CAFÉ BRÛLOT DIABOLIQUE

Make a pint and a half of coffee in any way you like (except perhaps in the Turkish manner) and keep it hot. In a deep silver bowl put eight cloves, one cinnamon stick, the peels of an orange and of a lemon cut in a thin ribbon and sugar to taste (your guests might like three tablespoons). Heat a quarter-pint of brandy, a ladle at a time, ignite and pour it over the ingredients in the bowl. Stir to dissolve the sugar. Pour in the hot coffee slowly and stir gently until the flames fade. You may also add a ladle of flaming Cointreau at this stage. Ladle the *café brûlot* into small, warmed cups.

COFFEE GROG

Pour a jigger each of light rum, brandy and Jamaica rum into a chafing dish. Add a ribbon of lemon and orange peel, six cloves and a sprinkling of cinnamon. Pour in a pint and a half of freshly made strong coffee. Stir and heat to near boiling point. Serve, adding sugar to taste and thick cream dribbled down the back of a spoon.

It is also good to pour the 'grog' over a teaspoonful of spiced butter placed at the bottom of a mug. This is made by creaming butter with brown sugar, a tiny pinch of salt and various ground spices such as cinnamon, nutmeg, allspice and ginger.

CAFÉ CARIOCA

In a chafing dish put one-and-a-half pints of freshly made strong coffee, sweetened to taste, and two peeled and sliced oranges (with the pith removed). Allow to rest with a cover for quarter of an hour, then heat till it just reaches boiling point. Add three jiggers of rum and stir. Pour into warmed cups, slipping two slices of orange in each. Top with whipped cream and sprinkle with grated orange rind, powdered chocolate or cinnamon.

Spirits and 'Pousse-Cafés'

There is no better way to conclude a fine meal than with brandy, served at the same time as the coffee. Without it a dinner composed of the most splendid dishes, accompanied by the noblest wines, remains incomplete. Coffee, small and black, high roasted and strong, provides a perfect complement. Together they facilitate digestion.

All the great spirits of the world find their place with coffee after a meal when they can be taken at leisure, in little sips, and their bouquet can be enjoyed.

There is Armagnac and the famous apple brandy of Normandy, Calvados. The list of *eaux-de-vie* produced from fruits and other plants in many parts of the world is endless, but the choice is not so vast for most tastes. Of these, Guillaumin made from pears, Kirsch from cherry stones, and Quetsch and Mirabelle from plums can be singled out. But for most, nothing can surpass the elusive complexity of Cognac, the depths and shallows, the high-lights and shades of its fragrance and savour.

There are, of course, the traditional '*pousse-cafés*', syrupy and prettily coloured, perfumed and spicy. Though many find their sweetness too cloying and their colour too pretty, it would be remiss in a book on coffee not to mention them. Aromatic liqueurs such as Kümmel based on caraway, and Chartreuse and Benedictine flavoured with herbs, are perhaps as good as the coffee liqueur, Tia Maria, and the chocolate one, Crème de Cacao. For those who like fruity flavours, orange Grand Marnier and Danish Cherry Heering are amongst the best of the many made with oranges, apricots, peaches, raspberries, black currants and cherries.

And from this side of the Channel there are the honeyed whiskies, Drambuie and Irish Mist, all after-dinner liquid sweet-meats to be enjoyed by the sweet-toothed after the sobering kick of coffee.

Friandises

A small bowl of home-made plum preserve arriving with my coffee on the Greek island of Skopelos last summer revived nostalgic longings for the *friandises* of the Orient; the dates in syrup, the crystallized orange peels and the assorted nut delights.

In the countries where once the Ottomans, the Moors or the

Arabs have been, it is usual to serve coffee with small sweet 'fancies' in the form of sweetmeats, jams or fruit preserves. Some of our restaurants have kept up the habit in a French version, a fashion which we would do well to adopt at home. Most of us long for a little sweetness at the end of a meal which has not been overloaded with rich desserts. Imagine also the delight of an unexpected visitor on being regaled with almond drops and apricot fancies instead of the ubiquitous biscuits.

As for the international repertoire of 'coffee cakes', it is vast and includes yeast cakes, richly filled and glazed cakes, dry pastries and *petits fours*, not to mention tarts and biscuits. To do them justice would mean filling a whole book. I would rather refer you to your own cookery books for these and for the preserves, which may be savoured by the teaspoon. You are more likely to find *friandises*, however, in your children's cook books where they seem to belong, if only for the ease with which they are made.

Here are a few of my favourites.

GLAZED GRAPES, TANGERINE OR ORANGE SECTIONS, CHERRIES OR GOOSEBERRIES

These must be made on the day that they are to be eaten. Choose ripe and tasty fruit in perfect condition. Any tears in the skin will result in a sticky glaze. Wash the fruit if necessary and let it dry completely. Tangerine and orange sections must be dried for a few hours. Make a syrup by bringing to the boil a quarter-pint of water with half a pound of sugar and a few drops of lemon juice. Simmer until a little syrup dropped into cold water becomes hard and brittle. Remove the pan from the heat but keep warm on a hot plate or in hot water so that the syrup glazes the fruit thinly. Keep stalks wherever possible so as to dip the fruit into the syrup, or use a fork. Place on a lightly oiled tray. The sparkling glaze will become hard at once. Serve on an elegant silver or glass dish.

ALMOND DROPS

These Middle Eastern delicacies are as simple to make as they are delicious. Mix one teacup of ground almonds and one teacup of icing sugar in a bowl. Add just enough orange blossom water to make a stiff paste. Knead until it is smooth. Shape into little balls the size of large marbles and roll in icing sugar. Decorate with blanched almond halves or pistachio nuts.

A superb variation is to stuff almond balls with finely chopped pistachios. Shape the paste into a ball, make a hole with your little finger and fill the hole with the nuts. Close over the pistachios, then roll into a ball again.

STUFFED DATES

Use a soft and juicy variety of dried dates. Make a slit in each. Remove the stone and stuff generously with the same paste as for almond drops.

STUFFED WALNUTS OR ALMOND DROPS

Sandwich two blanched almonds or two walnuts together with about one teaspoon of almond paste. Place on a lightly oiled tray. Make some caramel by heating sugar until it melts and becomes a golden colour. Pour over the stuffed nuts to bind them together.

APRICOT DROPS

Mince or finely chop half a pound of dried, slightly soft, apricots —a sharp rather than a sweet variety. Add a little icing sugar to taste and knead well to make a soft, smooth paste, wetting your hands occasionally. Work in two ounces of coarsely chopped pistachios. Shape into marble-sized balls and roll in icing sugar. Let them dry overnight.

CHOCOLATE TRUFFLES

Break five ounces of sweet chocolate into small pieces and melt in a bowl placed in boiling water. Finely chop or coarsely pulverize in a blender a quarter-pound of hazelnuts and stir into the melted chocolate. Remove from heat and blend in two ounces of soft butter cut into pieces. Add two tablespoons of rum, cognac or Bénédictine, and mix well. Put in the refrigerator until it is hard enough to shape. Roll marble-sized balls in powdered cocoa.

Iced Coffee

Having recently experienced Athens' hottest day for many years, I emerged convinced that few drinks are as refreshing as iced coffee. The original iced coffee was called Mazagran, probably after the Algerian fortress where the drink is said to have first become popular among French colonial troops in the North African deserts. It was made from coffee syrup and cold water.

A concentrated coffee syrup can be made which keeps a few months and which can serve as a base for iced drinks and any kind of coffee-flavoured drink or dessert. One pound of ground coffee with three-and-a-half pints of water will make a strong enough brew. Make it in any way you like, but strain it well or filter it if using a method which keeps the grounds. Add three pounds of sugar. Stir and bring to the boil. Pour into very clean, preferably sterilized bottles and seal. Store in a cool place to use when and as required. To serve iced coffee, dilute to taste in long glasses over ice cubes.

The innumerable versions served up throughout the world on request of iced coffee reveals a shadowiness of boundaries between the *cafés glacés*, the *refrescos de café*, the *frappés*, milk shakes, 'frosts', 'froths', 'floats' and 'nectars'. Chilled coffee can be served on ice cubes or with crushed ice or ice cream, and can be topped with whipped cream. Mixed with cream, which enhances iced coffee more than milk does, it is the celebrated *café Liégeois*.

Ways of making iced coffee are numerous, and in each case the same is true—that to make good iced coffee you must first make good hot coffee. Do not make it too long in advance (three hours at most); sweeten it or not, and simply allow it to cool in the refrigerator in a glass or china jug, covered to preserve as much of the aroma as possible, and so that it does not pick up any alien odour. If you will be using ice cubes which dilute the drink, make your coffee double strength using half the usual amount of water for the same amount of ground coffee. Allow this to cool, but not for too long, then pour it into a glass filled with an equal quantity of ice cubes. Ice cubes made by pouring fresh coffee into freezer trays add coolness without diluting the drink. Long glasses are attractive for serving.

Suitable additions include a strip or two of lemon peel. Fresh mint is also an excellent flavouring for cold coffee. Drop in a few leaves straight from your garden while the brew is cooling. Angostura bitters, popular in Italy, add a provocative taste, and rum is delightful too, as Brazilians well know. Pour a little into the chilled coffee just as you are about to serve it. And of course there are all the aromatics and the traditional companions; chocolate, honey and coconut, which are as good with cold as with hot coffee. A scoop of ice cream—vanilla, coffee or chocolate—will usually enhance any iced coffee. Here are a few popular recipes:

ICED COFFEE WITH MILK

'Café au lait' or Viennese Coffee may be put to cool in the refrigerator, covered—sweetened if you like. Serve topped with whipped cream. A little light cream may be preferred to milk. Otherwise, prepare double strength coffee and beat well with chilled milk in equal parts just before serving.

ICED SPICED COFFEE

For a largish quantity make about one-and-a-half pints of strong fresh coffee. Drop in four cinnamon sticks, eight cloves and eight allspice berries to steep while it cools, covered, in the refrigerator for at least an hour. Strain and serve over ice cubes. Sweeten to taste and garnish with whipped cream.

ICED COFFEE WITH HONEY

Pour freshly made strong coffee over a glassful of ice cubes with honey to taste (about a tablespoon will usually do). Top with whipped cream and dust with cinnamon and grated nutmeg.

ICED COFFEE MOCHA

Pour one-and-a-half pints of freshly made hot coffee over four tablespoons of powdered drinking chocolate or four ounces of chocolate (warmed up and melted in a saucepan), a little at first, and beating well until it is dissolved. Sweeten if you like, then chill, garnish with whipped cream and chocolate dust or shavings.

ICED COFFEE COCKTAIL

Make one-and-a-half pints of coffee and let it cool in a covered glass or china jug in the refrigerator with a long strip of lemon peel. Before serving, stir in a jigger or two of Crème de Cacao or Cognac. Pour into wine glasses over crushed ice or ice cubes with sugar to taste, or honey if you prefer. Dribble about a tablespoon of fresh cream off the back of a spoon into each glass.

COGNAC MOCHA

A delicious iced mixture of equal parts of very strong coffee, milk and Cognac, is French. An American version is made with evaporated milk and blended in a cocktail shaker.

❧CAFÉS FRAPPÉS☙

These South American favourites, usually called 'tropical delight' on menus, are truly delightful. *Frappés* are made with ice in a liquidizer, and blended until the texture is smooth, creamy and frothy. A lot of ice is used, sometimes as much ice as coffee. The coffee must be made strong accordingly, one-and-a-half times as strong or even double strength, that is, using half the usual quantity of water in brewing, so that it will not be too weak when combined with ice. Use a good blend for a flavoursome coffee. Sugar may be added while it is cooling in the liquidizer, according to taste. Fresh cream or ice cream are especially good blended into the *frappé* when the ice is already crushed. Serve the *frappé* immediately after it is made, as the froth soon subsides. If you like, top it with whipped cream.

SPICED COFFEE *FRAPPÉ*

Pour a pint of freshly brewed, extra strong coffee into a jug over two cinnamon sticks, four cloves and four allspice berries, cover and leave for at least one hour to cool in the refrigerator. Strain into a liquidizer, add a quarter-pint of cream and about six ice cubes. Blend to a creamy froth and serve immediately. In the same way, make honey, maple syrup or butterscotch *frappés* by adding any of these in the liquidizer. Omit the spices.

RUM AND COFFEE *FRAPPÉ*

Alcohol adds excitement to many *frappés*. This one is delicious. Blend one pint of chilled extra strong coffee with four ice cubes, three tablespoons of sugar or honey and three tablespoons of dark rum. When the ice is well crushed, add a quarter-pint of vanilla ice cream, blend a few seconds more, and serve immediately.

CAFÉ ALEXANDER

This is another very pleasant mixture. Pour one pint of extra strong chilled coffee into a liquidizer with three to four tablespoons of sugar, a quarter-pint of cream and three tablespoons each of brandy and Crème de Cacao liqueur. Drop in about six ice cubes and blend to a frothy cream. Serve at once.

INSTANT COFFEE MILK SHAKE

This drink, made with soluble coffee, has encouraged my children to drink milk for many years. In a liquidizer, blend one pint of milk, one tablespoon of instant coffee, three tablespoons of sugar and six ice cubes until all the ice has been crushed to a fine froth. Serve immediately.

MOKA HELADO

Pour three-quarters of a pint of hot freshly made coffee over three tablespoons of powdered drinking chocolate, or three ounces of chocolate (warmed and slightly melted). Pour a little at first and beat well to dissolve the chocolate properly. Chill, covered, in your refrigerator. Combine in a blender with half a pint of vanilla or coffee ice cream, and some sugar if you like. Serve at once.

COFFEE RUMBA

Blend three-quarters of a pint of chilled coffee in a liquidizer with half a pint of coffee ice cream, three to four tablespoons of rum and sugar to taste. Blend quickly and serve at once sprinkled with grated nutmeg. This is also good with Angostura bitters instead of rum.

COFFEE ICE CREAM SODA

Stir a quarter-pint of fresh single cream into three-quarters of a pint of chilled, strong, sweetened coffee in a jug. Pour into tall glasses, only half filling them. Add scoops of ice cream in each glass and fill with ice-cold soda water.

Coffee Ices

'Sorbet' and 'sherbet' are derived from the Arabic word, *sharbat*, for cold drink. Water ices are the most fragrant and delightful of foods to have been used as appetizers and digestives. They are still the interim course for soothing and revitalizing the stomachs of gourmands at London *barmitzvahs*, as they were at the feasts of ancient Rome. The history of water ices starts in the third century B.C. in China; they have come to us via the Middle East through Renaissance Italy.

GRANITA AL CAFFÉ

Granita al caffè con panna montata (with whipped cream) has remained the speciality of Italy, where people pour their sweetened left-over coffee into the freezer as soon as they have had enough. To make it, all you need is coffee, preferably a darkish roast, and sugar. However, mixing in a little egg white whipped to a firm snow makes for a less gritty consistency.

3–4 oz. finely ground coffee   *Serves 10*
7–8 oz. sugar
2 pints water
1 egg white, stiffly beaten

I like to use the greater quantity of coffee. The large amount of sugar is necessary, as otherwise the ice is hard and coarse. Put the water and sugar in a saucepan. Boil for a few minutes. Add the ground coffee to the boiling hot syrup and leave to infuse for ten minutes. Strain through a fine sieve or muslin, and cool. When it is cold, pour into a covered ice tray in the freezer. When it is partly frozen, turn it into a bowl, beat in the stiffly whisked egg white and return to the ice tray. Freeze until firm and smooth, beating every half-hour to break up the ice granules.

Serve with whipped cream. If you like, trickle a little rum, Cognac, Curaçao or Tia Maria over it. The use of a churn freezer will of course result in a smoother texture.

COFFEE CREAM ICE

The simplest of ice creams. Beat double cream until almost firm and flavour to taste with sugar and instant coffee dissolved in very little water. Add grated chocolate if you like, or a liqueur, before freezing. A coarsely crushed *pralin* (see method, *Mocha Praliné*, page 117) is also excellent.

PARFAIT AU CAFÉ

Light and creamy and as perfect as the name implies, the finest of all ice creams is made with cream and egg custard. Here are two versions. The first is my favourite.

First version: Serves 6
4 heaped tablespoons (1½ oz.) freshly roasted medium ground coffee
½ pint single cream
½ pint double cream
4 egg yolks
5 oz. sugar

Bring the single cream almost to the boil. Add the coffee, stir well and let it infuse for at least twenty minutes. Beat the sugar and the egg yolks in a bowl. Strain the cream through a fine sieve into the egg mixture and beat vigorously until well blended. Set the pan over boiling water and stir until the mixture thickens like a custard. Leave to cool. Whip the double cream until fairly stiff and fold into the cream custard. Freeze in an ice tray for three to four hours. Stir after an hour, bringing the frozen sides into the middle.

Second version: Serves 6
4 egg yolks
2 tablespoons instant coffee
4 oz. sugar
4 fl. oz. water
½ pint single cream
½ pint double cream

Beat the egg yolks and coffee in a bowl. Boil the sugar and water in a pan until the syrup thickens enough to coat a spoon. Let it cool a little, then slowly pour it over the egg mixture, beating vigorously. Set the bowl over boiling water and whisk until it thickens. Remove from the heat and let cool. Stir in the single cream. Whip the double cream until just firm and fold into the mixture. Pour into an ice tray and freeze for three or four hours, stirring occasionally after an hour, bringing the frozen sides into the middle.

There are many delicious variations to these basic coffee ice creams. You may add Tia Maria or Curaçao, or you may fold in grated chocolate or a chocolate sauce. Crushed burnt almonds or *pralin* (see method, *Mocha Praliné*, page 117) made with almonds or hazelnuts may be stirred into the custard before freezing. Chopped boiled chestnuts macerated in maraschino are delicious mixed into the ice cream before it is frozen. In France, scoops of these *parfaits* are often served on a bed of whipped cream and decorated with chocolate-covered coffee beans. An irresistible *coupe* called 'Jamaïque' is pineapple dice soaked in rum, covered with coffee ice and sprinkled with freshly pulverized coffee. Another, 'Clo-Clo', has broken *marrons glacés* soaked in maraschino at the bottom of the *coupe*. These are covered with coffee ice cream decorated with vanilla-flavoured whipped cream in which is embedded a single *marron*.

Try these, or some of the popular *bombe* combinations which match different ice creams. 'Madrilène' combines coffee praliné and vanilla, 'Mogador' is coffee and Kirsch, 'Mathilde' is coffee and apricot, 'Francillon' coffee and brandy and 'Zamora' coffee and Curaçao. These *bombes* are as seductive as their names.

Coffee Desserts and Cakes

Coffee plays a part in the aromatics of a remarkable variety of sweet dishes. It is indeed even used as a flavouring with meat, in a marinade for lamb, in sauces for pork or beef and in a glaze for cold meats, though not, I feel, successfully.

For those who would like to try a marinade, combine one coffee-cupful of strong coffee with half a cupful of wine vinegar and stir in two tablespoons of sugar, one tablespoon of mustard, one tablespoon Worcestershire sauce and a few drops of Tabasco. A leg of lamb may be rubbed with one rounded tablespoon of instant coffee mixed with salt and pepper, roasted in a slow oven and basted with some strong coffee. Minced meat may be moistened with strong coffee to make hamburgers, and meat balls may be poached in a liquor made with equal quantities of wine and strong coffee.

But for me, coffee is definitely a bean for the sweet dishes, like chocolate and the vanilla pod, both of which it happily weds. A good companion to most spirits and spices, it goes well with all the family of nuts, especially with the magnificent caramelized and crushed *pralines*. It gives a subtle surprise flavour to a few sauces and syrups for cooked fruits such as baked apples, fried bananas and stewed pears, or to serve with ice creams, mousses, puddings or soufflés. A quarter-pint of strong coffee boiled with half a pound of sugar until it is thick enough to coat a spoon is lovely, especially with rum or spices such as cinnamon, nutmeg or vanilla. Various cream sauces made with milk thickened with cornflour, flour or egg yolks find an original alternative with the addition of a little coffee.

A spoonful or two of coffee enriches many a chocolate, dried fruit, spice and nut cake, and a coffee filling is in the repertoire of most pastry enthusiasts, mixed with butter or egg yolks, as a custard or with fresh cream. An éclair is a special favourite, filled with a coffee-flavoured *crème patissière* and covered with coffee icing. Add a few tablespoons of strong coffee to a familiar cake. If the recipe does not call for extra liquid, instant coffee is better used.

Coffee is naturally at its best in the uncooked cold dishes, the jellies and mousses, and the lightly cooked custards and creams made with milk, cream, eggs and butter. Here the aroma and flavour of freshly made coffee are fully preserved, so use a good blend. A high roast gives an extra kick, but with milk or cream it is better to use a medium or light roast.

Delightfully refreshing for an *al fresco* luncheon in the garden or to conclude a rich meal, coffee jellies should certainly not be confined to the nursery and might even be labelled 'adult flavoured' by the gelatine manufacturers. It is important to make them from fine beans. The liquor must be crystal clear and grounds must be banished by filtering through a paper filter or a fine strainer.

Besides the well-known dishes to which coffee offers an original variation, there are, of course, the special coffee dishes, many of them celebrated under the name of 'Mocha' after the Yemeni port, which have been evolved around the special qualities of coffee. I offer some favourites that have come my way.

COFFEE SYRUP

Into a sugar syrup made by boiling half a pound of sugar and a quarter-pint of water, stir two teaspoons of instant coffee and four tablespoons of cocoa, and cook a little while longer.

COFFEE SAUCE

Beat two eggs. Add a quarter-pint of strong hot coffee gradually, beating well. Add a pinch of salt and two ounces of sugar, and stir over boiling water until the sauce thickens. Do not let it curdle. Chill. Just before serving, fold in a quarter-pint of thick whipped cream.

CHOCOLATE AND COFFEE SAUCE

Melt a quarter-pound of sweet chocolate broken into pieces in one fluid ounce of strong coffee and stir well. Let it cool and add two ounces of butter, a little at a time, beating until it is thoroughly blended.

MOCHA BUTTER CREAM

A filling for cakes. Beat two egg yolks with three ounces of icing sugar in a bowl until pale and creamy. Continue to beat over boiling water until the cream has thickened. Dissolve two tablespoons of instant coffee in two tablespoons of rum and beat well into the egg mixture. Remove from the heat. Stir in while still warm three ounces of unsalted butter in little pieces, one at a time, beating until well blended.

If you prefer not to use rum, dissolve the coffee in water or milk instead.

RICOTTA AL CAFFÉ

Elizabeth David's lovely recipe for cream cheese with coffee. For four people allow eight to ten ounces of cream cheese, four to six ounces of caster sugar, four dessertspoonfuls of freshly roasted coffee very finely ground (as for Turkish coffee), and two fluid ounces of rum. Put the cream cheese through a sieve; add the sugar, the coffee and the rum and stir it until it is smooth and thick. Make the cream at least two hours before serving, so that the coffee flavour has time to develop. Keep it in a cold place. Serve it with, if possible, fresh cream and thin wafer biscuits. I prefer to use only two dessertspoonfuls of a dark roast.

ST. VALENTINE'S CREAM   *Serves 3–5*

A lighter cream. Beat a quarter-pound of cream cheese (or 'petits suisses') with two egg yolks, two dessertspoons of sugar and the same amount of cream. Add one level tablespoon of medium roasted and pulverized fresh ground coffee or one teaspoon of instant coffee and mix well. Fold in two stiffly beaten egg whites. Served chilled in little pots.

BLACK COFFEE JELLY

Make a pint of fresh strong brew with a darkish roast. Filter or strain and sweeten to taste while still hot. Sprinkle with half an ounce (one rounded tablespoon) of unflavoured gelatine and stir until completely dissolved. Pour into wineglasses or glass bowls where the rich colour can be enjoyed. Chill until it sets. Serve topped with sweet whipped cream.

For a spicy alternative, brew the coffee with one teaspoonful of cinnamon, a pinch of nutmeg, three cloves and two cracked cardamom pods before filtering.

COFFEE CREAM JELLY   *Serves 6*

This is one I have just made and loved its special texture. Make half a pint of double strength coffee using four heaped tablespoons of a medium roast. Filter or strain the liquor. Add two to three tablespoons of sugar and half an ounce (one rounded tablespoon) of unflavoured gelatine and stir well until dissolved, putting the container over boiling water if necessary. Chill in the refrigerator until it has almost set. Whip half a pint of thick cream, then whip the coffee jelly with a whisk or rotary beater until it is frothy and stir both well together. Pour the jelly mixture into a wetted mould and leave to set in the refrigerator for three or four hours.

You may like to vary this recipe by adding two or three table-spoons of a spirit such as Cognac or rum.

COFFEE MOUSSE   *Serves 6*

A light and fragrant dessert. Make a fresh, extra strong quarter-pint of coffee using three heaped tablespoons of a medium roast. While this is still hot, stir in half an ounce of powdered un-flavoured gelatine until dissolved. Beat three egg yolks with three or four tablespoons of sugar in a bowl over a pan of hot water until thick and creamy. Remove from the pan and continue to beat until it has cooled. Gradually stir in the coffee and gelatine mixture and a quarter-pint of single cream, and beat well. Whisk the three egg whites until they are stiff, then gently fold into the coffee mixture. Pour into a wet mould and chill until it is set.

This mousse may also be scented with a vanilla pod. Other excellent alternative additions are rum, Kirsch and Cognac.

MOCHA *PRALINÉ*   *Serves 12*

This *diplomate* has been my father's favourite birthday cake ever since I can remember. We give the recipe to all those who say they cannot make cakes, as this one simply cannot fail. They also find it magnificent.

¼ lb. hazelnuts
5 tablespoons caster sugar
½ pint double cream
¼ pint single cream
1 heaped tablespoon instant coffee
3 packets *boudoirs* (16 × 3 biscuits)
Café au lait

First make a *pralin* with the hazelnuts as follows: brown them lightly by rolling them in a frying pan over medium heat. When the skins begin to loosen, remove from the heat. When cool enough, rub the nuts between your hands (one way of removing the flaking skins is to blow them out of the pan through a window, or better still, go out in the garden). Add three tablespoons of sugar and return the pan to the fire. When the sugar is melted and lightly browned, stir and coat all the hazelnuts. Pour on to a lightly oiled tray. When it is cool, break the nut brittle into pieces. Keep a few whole caramelized hazelnuts for a garnish. Pound the rest in a mortar or put them for a few seconds in a blender.

Next, beat the double cream and single cream together, being careful not to overbeat or the mixture may turn to butter. Add two tablespoons of caster sugar and one tablespoon of instant coffee dissolved in a tablespoon of warm milk. Moisten the *boudoirs* by dipping them a few seconds in café au lait or milk flavoured with a little instant coffee (a friend adds a Mexican coffee liqueur, Kahlúa—an excellent alternative. Tia Maria may also be used.) Do not let them soak up too much liquid or they will become soggy. Start by putting a layer of *boudoirs* in a round or square mould (an eight-inch one would be fine) with a loose base or detachable sides. Spread with a thin layer of cream and sprinkle with a little *pralin*. Repeat the layers until all the *boudoirs* are used up, ending with a good layer of cream. Lift out the *diplomate* from the base or remove the sides of the mould. Spread a little of the coffee cream around the sides. Sprinkle all over with *pralin* and place a few whole caramelized nuts on the top of the gateâu.

This cake freezes very well. Just out of the freezer it is like a *semi-freddo* ice cream.

PORC-ÉPIC

Another French *gâteau mocha* which we used to call *porc-épic* (porcupine) because of the spiky almonds all over the top, is made with a butter cream instead of fresh cream.

6 oz. unsalted butter
2½ oz. caster sugar

2 egg yolks
2 level tablespoons instant coffee
2 tablespoons hot water
whole burnt almonds for decoration
2 packets *boudoirs* (16 × 2 biscuits)

Cream the butter and sugar together. Add the egg yolks and blend
well. Add the instant coffee dissolved in the two tablespoons of
hot water. Beat till light and fluffy. Moisten the *boudoirs* in strong
black coffee, with a little rum if you like. Alternate layers of these
with butter cream as in previous recipe. Decorate generously with
burnt almonds.

FROZEN COFFEE MOUSSE *PRALINEÉ*   Serves 6–8

No dessert better demonstrates the affinity of coffee and *praliné*.
   Make a coarsely crushed or chopped *pralin* (see *Mocha Praliné*,
page 117) with a quarter-pound of hazelnuts or almonds caramelized in three or four tablespoons of sugar. Then make a mousse
with:

4 eggs
6 tablespoons caster sugar
3 teaspoons powdered instant coffee
½ pint double cream

Separate the egg whites and yolks into different bowls. Whip the
egg whites very stiff and beat in two tablespoons of sugar. Beat the
yolks with the remaining sugar until pale and creamy. Continue
to beat over hot water until the cream has thickened. Stir in the
instant coffee, remove from the heat and incorporate the *pralin*.
Allow to cool. Whip the double cream until almost firm and
fold into the coffee mixture. Very carefully fold in the stiff egg
whites. Pour gently into an attractive, wetted mould and freeze
for at least an hour before serving. Dip for a second into hot water
and unmould. Pour a chocolate and coffee sauce (page 115) over it,
and serve.

MOCHA MOUSSE   *Serves 6–8*

A chocolate mousse with a taste of coffee.

4 oz. bitter chocolate
¼ pint water
4 tablespoons ground coffee
6 oz. caster sugar
5 eggs
1 tablespoon Cognac or coffee liqueur

Melt the chocolate, broken into squares, in the top of a double
boiler. Make a concentrated coffee by just bringing the water to
the boil with the coffee and allowing it to infuse. Strain and stir
in the sugar. Add this to the chocolate in the double boiler. Stir
until well blended. Separate the egg yolks from the whites. Add
the yolks, one at a time, beating vigorously. Remove from the
heat quickly when the sauce thickens slightly, and add Cognac.
Beat the egg whites stiff and fold into the chocolate mixture when
it is only just warm. Pour into small individual bowls and chill
overnight.

A delightful alternative is to stir a little *pralin* (see method,
Mocha Praliné, page 117) into the mousse.

BAVAROISE AU CAFÉ   *Serves 6–8*

Perhaps the loveliest of all the coffee creams.

1 pint milk
5 heaped tablespoons pale roast ground coffee
5 egg yolks
4 oz. caster sugar
½ oz. gelatine (1 tablespoon)
¼ pint double cream
3 tablespoons Cognac—optional

Bring the milk to the boil. Stir in the ground coffee and leave to
infuse for about twenty minutes. Strain. Whisk the eggs in a

bowl. Add the sugar gradually and whisk well until pale and creamy. Slowly beat in the hot milk. Transfer to a saucepan over medium heat and stir with a wooden spoon until the mixture has thickened into a custard. Remove from the heat. Add the gelatine, dissolved in two tablespoons of hot water, and beat into the hot custard. Leave to cool a little in the refrigerator.

Beat the cream until firm and gently fold into the custard. Stir in a little Cognac if you like. Pour into a lightly oiled mould. Chill in the refrigerator for three to four hours, until firm. Unmould and serve with a chocolate sauce poured over it.

For the sauce: Melt four ounces of unsweetened chocolate over boiling water. Add eight or nine fluid ounces of cream and three ounces of caster sugar and stir well. Flavour if you like with a little vanilla, a quarter-teaspoon of cinnamon or a tablespoon of rum. Add about an ounce of chopped almonds. Chill.

CHARLOTTE RUSSE   Serves 6–8

Line a lightly oiled mould with *madeleines* or *boudoirs* moistened slightly by dipping in black coffee mixed with dark rum or Cognac. Half fill with the same custard as for *Bavaroise au café*. Sprinkle with about two ounces of chopped burnt almonds. Cover with a layer of moistened *boudoirs* or *madeleines* and pour the rest of the bavaroise cream over the top. Chill in the refrigerator for three or four hours. Unmould and serve with the above chocolate sauce.

CRÉME SAINTE-HONORÉ AU CAFÉ   Serves 6–8

1 pint milk
3–4 tablespoons ground coffee
6 oz. granulated sugar
5 eggs
2½ oz. sifted flour
1 tablespoon caster sugar
2 tablespoons coffee liqueur or rum (optional)

Beat the egg yolks and sugar for two or three minutes until pale yellow and creamy. Add the flour and beat well. Bring the milk to the boil with the ground coffee. Stir and leave to infuse for a few minutes. Pour very gradually through a strainer over the egg yolk mixture, beating all the time until well blended. Pour into a heavy-bottomed saucepan and place over a moderate heat. Stir constantly with a wooden spoon until the mixture thickens. Use a whisk or electric beater if it becomes lumpy. When it begins to boil continue to stir over very low heat for two to three minutes to allow the flour to cook. Be careful that the cream does not burn at the bottom of the pan. If you like, add two tablespoons of coffee liqueur or rum to this *crème patissière*. Beat the egg whites with a pinch of salt until stiff. Add one tablespoon of caster sugar and continue to beat until peaks are formed. Fold, a little at a time to begin with, into the hot cream. Chill in the refrigerator.

You may stir in two ounces of *pralin* (see method, *Mocha Praliné*, page 117) with the egg whites as a delicious alternative. For a Mocha version, beat two ounces of chocolate melted with the coffee liqueur, into the hot cream.

CHARLOTTE MALAKOFF AU CAFÉ   Serves 12 or more

½ lb. softened unsalted butter
6 oz. caster sugar
1 egg yolk
6 oz. ground almonds or ground walnuts, or a mixture of both, or
    praliné hazelnuts (see *Mocha Praliné*, page 117)
⅛ pint coffee made with 3 tablespoons ground coffee
¾ pint cream (whipping or a mixture of single and double)
40 sponge fingers
1 small glass rum, coffee liqueur or Cognac
milk (about ½ pint)
toasted split almonds

Cream butter and sugar for three or four minutes until soft. Beat in the egg yolk and the coffee until a smooth cream. Stir in the ground almonds or walnuts. Beat three-quarters of a pint of whipping cream, or a half-pint of double and a quarter-pint of single cream, until stiff and fold into the almond and coffee mixture.

Line a round cake tin (about three inches high and eight inches in diameter) with greaseproof paper. Dip the sponge fingers in the milk mixed with the rum, Cognac or liqueur for a few seconds only. Turn them over once and do not let them become saturated. Line the bottom and sides of the tin with them. Turn half of the almond and coffee cream into the lined mould. Arrange a layer of the sponge fingers over it. Repeat with another layer of cream and sponge fingers. Trim the tops of sponge fingers lining the sides if necessary. Cover with greaseproof paper. Put in the refrigerator for a few hours at least, preferably overnight, before serving. The cream must be chilled firm.

Remove the greaseproof paper. Run a knife around the inside of the mould and turn the dessert out on to a serving dish. Peel the greaseproof paper from the top and return to the refrigerator until serving time. Decorate if you like with toasted split almonds, and serve with whipped cream.

CHARLOTTE BASQUE AU MOCHA   Serves 12 or more

This *charlotte* is made in the same way as the *Malakoff*. The whipped cream is substituted by a custard in which three ounces of plain chocolate has been melted. Make a coffee *crème patissière* as for the *Crème Saint-Honoré au café*. Break the chocolate into small pieces and stir it into the custard until it is well blended. Let it cool well before you beat it into the almond cream. As this *crème patissière* already has coffee, do not add any to the butter and almond cream.

POTS DE CRÈME À LA JAVANAISE   Serves 6

1 pint milk
3 tablespoons medium roast ground coffee
3 tablespoons sugar

3 egg yolks
1 whole egg

Bring the milk to the boil with the ground coffee and allow to infuse a few minutes. Strain. Stir in the sugar. In a bowl, lightly beat together the three egg yolks and one whole egg. Gradually pour in the milk, beating well. Pour the custard into ramekins. Place in a *bain marie* (a pan with water reaching up to two-thirds of the height of the pots). Bake in a preheated moderately slow oven (325° F. gas 3) for about 45 minutes or until the cream has set.

For *Pots de Crème au Mocha*, melt two ounces of chocolate, broken into pieces, in the milk at the same time as the sugar.

MOCHA SOUFFLÉ   *Serves 4*

¼ pint milk
3 tablespoons ground coffee
1 oz. butter
1 oz. flour (scant measure)
1 oz. bitter chocolate
2 tablespoons rum or coffee liqueur
3 egg yolks
4 egg whites

Bring the milk to the boil with the ground coffee. Leave for a few minutes and strain. Melt the butter. Stir in the flour and combine. Add the warm milk and stir until well blended. Add the chocolate, broken into small squares, and stir until melted. Remove from the heat. Drop in the egg yolks, beating vigorously. At this point the mixture may be kept for a few hours. The egg whites may then be beaten and added just before serving. Beat the egg whites with a pinch of salt until they form stiff peaks. Fold lightly into the mixture and turn into a well-buttered and sugared two-and-a-half pint soufflé dish. Cook in a preheated oven at 400° F. (gas 6) for about half an hour. Test with a skewer. If dry, serve immediately.

ELIZABETH DAVID'S COFFEE CHESTNUTS

For four people you need about thirty-six shelled and skinned chestnuts. Put them in a pan with enough water to cover and two tablespoons of sugar. Simmer until they are soft. In another pan (preferably a double saucepan) put the yolks of two eggs, a tablespoon of sugar, a teacup of strong black coffee, two tablespoons of cream or top of the milk and a liqueur glass of rum. Stir the sauce over a low flame until it thickens and pour it over the strained chestnuts in a silver dish.

Coffee goes well with chestnuts and its flavour will enhance most purées, compotes or gâteaux. Whether you use fresh cream, *crème anglaise* or just sugar, you simply add a little strong freshly made coffee or instant coffee powder.

Chestnuts are also excellent poached whole in a sugar syrup flavoured with a little coffee.

MERINGUE LAYER CAKE   *Serves 10*

This magnificent cake is made up of 3 rounds of meringue sandwiched together with a coffee butter cream.

For the meringue:
4 egg whites
a pinch of salt
8 oz. caster sugar

Preheat the oven to 250° F. (gas ½). Draw three circles about eight or nine inches in diameter on pieces of greaseproof paper and place on baking sheets. Beat the egg whites (which should be at room temperature). Add a pinch of salt when they begin to froth. Keep beating and when they form soft peaks add two tablespoons of sugar. Continue to beat until they form stiff shining peaks. Fold in the rest of the sugar quickly, a tablespoon at a time, with a spatula. Divide the meringue out on to the three circles on the greaseproof papers and spread evenly to fill the circles with the spatula. Bake gently in the oven for an hour and a half, until the meringues are slightly coloured and crisp. Leave in the oven to dry out. Peel off the paper when they are cool. If they are not to be used at once, keep in a sealed box.

For the cream:
3 oz. granulated sugar
3 fl. oz. (about 6 tablespoons) water
2 tablespoons ground coffee
4 egg yolks
¼ lb. unsalted butter

Bring the water to the boil with the ground coffee. Let it rest for a few minutes and strain. Bring the coffee and sugar to the boil in a clean pan and cook gently on a low flame until the syrup has thickened enough to coat a spoon and forms a thread when tested in cold water. Beat the yolks until creamy in a bowl. Slowly add the hot syrup, a little at a time and beating constantly. Continue beating until the mixture has cooled, over cold water if you like. Cream the butter and gradually beat in the egg mixture. Cool in the refrigerator for an hour before using. Spread the butter cream between the meringue layers and around the sides and cover the top of the cake. Garnish the cake with toasted flaked almonds.

A coffee meringue and a nut meringue are delicious variations. For a coffee meringue fold in one teaspoon of instant powdered coffee with the sugar. For a nut meringue fold in a quarter-pound of ground toasted hazelnuts mixed with one tablespoon of corn-flour with the sugar, being careful not to deflate the egg whites. In this case, bake a further half hour in the oven. Thick, sweetened whipped cream flavoured slightly with instant coffee powder is a nice alternative to the butter cream.

WALNUT AND COFFEE CAKE   *Serves 8*

This unusual recipe for a richly textured cake was given to me by a Polish lady.

4 eggs
6 oz. walnuts, coarsely chopped
4 oz. icing sugar
1 tablespoon powdered drinking chocolate
1 tablespoon pulverized ground coffee
1 tablespoon fine breadcrumbs

Separate yolks and whites. Cream the egg yolks and sugar. Add
breadcrumbs, coffee and chocolate powder and combine thoroughly.
Add the walnuts and mix well. Gently fold in the stiffly beaten
egg whites and pour into a cake tin (about eight-inch diameter)
which has been greased with butter and dusted with flour. Bake
in a preheated 350° F. (gas 4) oven for 45 minutes. When the
cake is cool, turn out and spread with a butter cream made with:

$\frac{1}{4}$ lb. unsalted butter
$\frac{1}{4}$ lb. icing sugar
1 egg yolk
2 tablespoons very strong coffee, made by pouring 2 tablespoons
    of boiling water over a heaped tablespoon of ground coffee
    and straining.

Cream the butter and sugar. Add the egg yolk and the coffee, and
beat well to a smooth cream.

COFFEE AND ALMOND *TORTE*   *Serves 10–12*

6 oz. ground almonds
4 oz. self-raising flour
6 oz. sugar
4 eggs
2 tablespoons instant coffee

Separate the egg yolks and whites. Beat the yolks and sugar together until creamy. Add the instant coffee and the ground

almonds. Beat the egg whites until stiff and gently fold alternately with the flour into the almond and yolk mixture. Grease a ten-inch diameter cake tin and dust with flour. Pour the cake mix into it and bake in a preheated moderate 350° F. (gas 4) oven for about 30 to 45 minutes. When it is cool, turn out and split into two layers. Fill and cover it with Mocha cream made with:

4 oz. sugar
2 tablespoons instant coffee
2 egg yolks
2 tablespoons butter

Melt the butter and sugar together in a saucepan. When the sugar is quite dissolved, add the coffee and beat in the egg yolks. Remove the saucepan from the heat and beat thoroughly until the mixture is cool and creamy.

CHESTNUT GÂTEAU   *Serves 6–8*

1 lb. chestnuts
1 pint milk
3 tablespoons ground coffee
6 oz. sugar
3 egg whites
3 tablespoons sugar

With a sharp knife make an incision on the flat side of each chestnut. Plunge the chestnuts into boiling water and boil for ten minutes. Pour away the water, and while they are still hot peel off the shell. Bring the milk to the boil with the ground coffee. Allow to infuse for a few minutes and strain. Cook the chestnuts in this milk with the sugar for about forty minutes. Put through a food mill or liquidizer. Make a caramel sauce by melting the three tablespoons of sugar and allowing it to turn brown. Add two tablespoons of water and stir until the caramel has melted. Pour into a mould (a round *savarin* tin will do well) and turn it around until the caramel has coated all the inside. Beat the egg whites until stiff and fold into the chestnuts. Pour into the coated mould. Place in a pan of hot water and cook forty-five minutes in a 325° F. (gas 2½) oven. Turn mould upside down on to a dish. Serve cold garnished with whipped cream.

Further Reading

BRAMAH, Edward. *Tea and Coffee: A Modern View of 300 Years of Tradition*, Hutchinson, 1972.

DUFOUR (Lyon). Treatise on The Manner of Making Coffee, Tea and Chocolate (*Traités nouveaux et curieux du Café*), 1684.

ROBINSON, Edward. *The Early English Coffee House*, Dolphin Press, 1972. (First Edition 1893.)

SCHAPIRA, Joel, David and Karl. *The Book of Coffee and Tea*, St. Martin's Press, New York, 1975.

SIVETZ, M. and FOOTE, H. *Coffee Processing Technology* (2 vols.), A.V.I. Publishing Co., Westport, Connecticut, 1963.

UKERS, William H. *All About Coffee*, The Tea and Coffee Trade Journal Co., New York, 1935.

URIBE, C. Andres. *Brown Gold*, Random House, New York, 1954.

Weights and Measures, Temperatures

WEIGHTS AND MEASURES

Approximate Metric Equivalents of Avoirdupois Weights
N.B. These figures are proportional and are worked out to the nearest round figure.

Weight

1 oz.	= 28·5 grammes
4 oz.	= 114 grammes
8 oz.	= 225·5 grammes
1 lb.	= 450 grammes
1 lb. 1½ oz.	= 500 grammes (½ kilogram)
2 lb. 3 oz.	= 1,000 grammes (1 kilogram)

Approximate Metric Equivalents of British Measures of Capacity

1 gill or 5 fluid oz.	= 0·142 litre
4 gills or 20 fluid oz. or 1 pint	= 0·568 litre
1¾ pints	= 1 litre
2 pints or 1 quart	= 1·136 litres

OVEN TEMPERATURES
(approximate equivalents)

Degrees Centigrade	Gas setting	Electric setting (Fahrenheit)
110	$\frac{1}{4}$	225
120	$\frac{1}{2}$	250
140	1	275
150	2	300
160	3	325
180	4	350
190	5	375
200	6	400
220	7	425
230	8	450
240	9	475

Water boils at 212° F. or 100° C.

Index

Numerals in **bold** refer to illustrations

MORE ABOUT PENGUINS
AND PELICANS

For further information about books available from Penguins please write to Dept EP, Penguin Books Ltd, Harmondsworth, Middlesex UB7 0DA.

In the U.S.A.: For a complete list of books available from Penguins in the United States write to Dept CS, Penguin Books, 625 Madison Avenue, New York, New York 10022.

In Canada: For a complete list of books available from Penguins in Canada write to Penguin Books Canada Ltd, 2801 John Street, Markham, Ontario L3R 1B4.

In Australia: For a complete list of books available from Penguins in Australia write to the Marketing Department, Penguin Books Australia Ltd, P.O. Box 257, Ringwood, Victoria 3134.

In New Zealand: For a complete list of books available from Penguins in New Zealand write to the Marketing Department, Penguin Books (NZ) Ltd, P.O. Box 4019, Auckland 10.

Also by Claudia Roden

A Book of Middle Eastern Food

'The cuisine of the Middle East has, for some mysterious reason, remained practically unexplored, but now that we can buy most of the ingredients here, we have an opportunity – encouraged by Claudia Roden – to try it for ourselves. This is a book for those wishing to widen their cookery knowledge and add new variety to the dinner table. Particularly good are the set-the-scene introductions to each recipe, and the section on origins and influences. And the dietary laws are useful for those who entertain overseas visitors. It makes fascinating reading'– *Good Housekeeping*.

More delicious cookery in Penguins!

From Julia Child's Kitchen

'Julia Child may be the most important person in the world of food' – Paul Levy in the *Observer*

'French bread, croissants, vacherins, quiches, crab dishes, good homely vegetables and soups, even the most elaborate dish achieves a startling simplicity when subjected to Julia Child's genius' – *Daily Telegraph*

Food with the Famous
Jane Grigson

Part cookery book, part social history, and always an unqualified delight, *Food with the Famous* relates cookery to life beyond the kitchen. Through recipes of their favourite dishes, Jane Grigson introduces us to such famous people as John Evelyn, Jane Austen, Proust and Zola.

More For Your Money
Shirley Goode and Erica Griffiths

'This collection of recipes and ideas aims to cut your weekly food budget but also to give you meals which are something special. It gives you the chance to challenge galloping inflation with hints on costing, using convenience foods and fuel saving so that the next price rise becomes a chance to show off your ingenuity instead of another crushing blow' – The Authors

More delicious cookery in Penguins!

Easy Cooking for Three or More
Louise Davies

Easy recipes for busy cooks – an invaluable, practical guide to family meals that shows you how to save time and impress without losing any of the flavour.

The Philosopher in the Kitchen
Jean-Anthelme Brillat-Savarin

Back in print after a long absence, *The Philosopher in the Kitchen* is quite without precedent. First published in 1825, it is a unique combination of recipes, aphorisms, reflections, reminiscences, history and philosophy that has helped to place gastronomy among the highest arts.

The Vegetarian Epicure
Anna Thomas

The answer to all those who consider vegetarian food boring and fit only for rabbits. In Anna Thomas's imaginative and skilful hands vegetarian cookery becomes a rich, exciting and varied way of eating that should appeal not only to the confirmed vegetarian but to the confirmed meat-eater as well.

Cooking in a Bedsitter
Katharine Whitehorn

Equipment, stores, cooking times and about 300 recipes – both Cooking to Stay Alive and Cooking to Impress – are covered in this excellent book. It's a survival guide for those cooking in limited space, with little time and less money, and an absolute 'must' for anyone with the sneaking suspicion that all those baked beans, etc., can't really be *healthy*!

Clementine Churchill

Mary Soames

Lady Soames describes her book as 'a labour of love – but I trust not of blind love'; others have acclaimed it as one of the outstanding biographies of the decade:

'Perceptive and affectionate, shrewd and tender . . . a joy to read' – Elizabeth Longford

'Lady Soames has carried out the extremely delicate and difficult task of writing the real story of her mother. I found it particularly moving because I had a very deep affection for her father and mother' – Harold Macmillan

A Portrait of Jane Austen

David Cecil

David Cecil's magnificent and highly enjoyable portrait of a writer who represents for us, as no other, the elegance, grace and wit of Georgian England.

'A masterpiece which ought to be in every educated home. Nobody could have done it better, nobody will be able to do it so well again. The book is a monument to subject and author' – Auberon Waugh in *Books and Bookmen*

Charmed Lives

Michael Korda

The story of Alexander Korda and the fabulous Korda film dynasty starring Garbo, Dietrich, Churchill and a cast of thousands.

'Charmed lives, doubly charmed book . . . Comments, jokes, experiences; and at the heart of it all there is Alexander Korda, powerful, brilliant, extravagant, witty, charming. And fortunate: fortunate in his biographer. Few men have the luck to be written about with so personal an appreciation, so amused, yet so deep an affection' – Dilys Powell in *The Times*

Look out for these in Penguins!

Carnival in Romans
A People's Uprising at Romans 1579–1580

Emmanuel Le Roy Ladurie

'In February 1580, Carnival in Romans was a time of masks and massacres for the divided citizenry.' Concentrating on two colourful and bloody weeks, the author of *Montaillou* vividly resurrects the social and political events that led to the tragedy of 1580.

'This is a book not to be missed' – Christopher Hill

The View in Winter
Reflections on Old Age

Ronald Blythe

'Old age is not an emancipation from desire for most of us; that is a large part of its tragedy. The old want their professional status back or their looks ... most of all they want to be wanted.' Ronald Blythe listened to all kinds of people who are in and around their eighties as they talked about their old age, to make this marvellous, haunting record of an experience that touches us all.

'It deserves, like *Akenfield*, to become a classic'– A. Alvarez in the *Observer*

The Old Patagonian Express
By Train through the Americas

Paul Theroux

From blizzard-stricken Boston to arid Patagonia; travelling by luxury express and squalid local trucks; sweating and shivering by turns as the temperature and altitude shot up and down; Paul Theroux's vivid pen clearly evokes the contrasts of a journey 'to the end of the line'.

'One of the most entrancing travel books written in our time' – C. P. Snow in the *Financial Times*

The Americans
Letters from America 1969–1979

Alistair Cooke

With his engaging blend of urbanity and charm, Alistair Cooke talks about Watergate and Christmas in Vermont, gives opinions on jogging and newspaper jargon, creates memorable cameos of Americans from Duke Ellington to Groucho Marx and discusses a host of other topics – all in that relaxed, anecdotal style which has placed him among our best-loved radio broadcasters.

'One of the most gifted and urbane essayists of the century, a supreme master' – Benny Green in the *Spectator*

The White Album
Joan Didion

In this scintillating epitaph to the sixties Joan Didion exposes the realities and mythologies of her native California – observing a panorama of subjects and ranging from Manson to bikers to Black Panthers to the Women's Movement to John Paul Getty's museum, the Hoover Dam and Hollywood.

'A richly worked tapestry of experiences' – Rachel Billington

The Seventies
Christopher Booker

From the rise of Mrs Thatcher to the murder of Lord Mount-batten, from the energy crisis to the trial of Jeremy Thorpe, from the Cult of Nostalgia to the Collapse of the Modern Movement in the Arts . . . In this series of penetrating essays Christopher Booker explores the underlying themes which shaped our thoughts and our lives in the 'seventies.

'Booker is quite compulsive' – *Punch*

'Constantly stimulating . . . savagely funny' – *Evening Standard*